This volume reads like a roll call
of giant figures of Old Testament history:
Abraham . . . Moses . . . Joshua . . . Samuel . . .
Saul . . . David . . . Solomon and others who loom
large in the heritage of western civilization.
This study of their lives,
their lands, and their armies
forms a fascinating backdrop to modern
problems of the Near East.
For the fruits of ancient enmities force
their way into current newspaper headlines,
strongly affect foreign policies
of world powers, and ominously thrust
a long arm into accounts of
political assassination in America.
"Wanderers, Slaves and Kings" takes the
reader back to origins and lets him
make his own applications to modern history.
But it does more. It points
to one who stands astride all history
as the uniquely dominant figure:
Jesus Christ, Son of David, Son of God.

wanderers, slaves & kings

DAILY DEVOTIONS AND BIBLE STUDIES

by Manford George Gutzke

A Division of G/L Publications
Glendale, California, U.S.A.

Published by
Regal Books Division, G/L Publications
Glendale, California 91205, U.S.A.

Library of Congress Catalogue Card No. 71-78549

CONTENTS

Foreword

This book may be used as an elective Sunday School
course, or for Sunday evening fellowships or midweek
Bible study classes.

A study guide is available for use with this book. Consult
your supplier or the publisher.

FOREWORD

The famous men and events of early biblical history have had a measureless impact upon subsequent history down to our own day. And the mere mention of a name like Michelangelo suffices as a reminder of their large-scale invasion of the arts across the centuries. And the names of Milton and Bunyan bespeak the depth of the literary imprint.

But basic to these effects and more profound than all of them has been that upon individual men and women through the centuries. For the Old Testament is the greatest example of pictorial teaching in terms of history and biography ever given to mankind. There is Moses with his Law and his leadership. David, almost larger than life in his sublime virtues which render shocking by contrast his gross passions. And there is Solomon reflecting in his life the transcendent glory of Israel's Golden Age being gradually undermined by base and abominable corruption.

Before these figures is Abraham, who "staggered not at the promise of God through unbelief, but was strong in faith, giving glory to God." And this is what *Wanderers, Slaves and Kings* is basically about: the life of faith in God. The Lord chooses a covenant people to serve Him in love in response to His forgiving love for them, which pursues them through their recurring disobedience and rebellion even to making them the means of sending to earth His Son, our Saviour.

This volume is the first in a series of four, which will carry the reader through both Old and New

Testaments, delineating the practical lessons of living by faith and how they apply to modern life and problems. In all the volumes Jesus Christ is exalted as the one who gives significance to history, and His cross set forth as the truly decisive point for all of time and eternity.

How to Use This Book

This is a daily devotional and study workbook. Here are some suggestions for its most profitable use.

Study the Scriptures daily, using the Bible readings in this book as your guide. There are Bible readings for every day of the week. Always begin by asking the Holy Spirit to guide you and give you a personal message for the day. Read with a pencil in your hand and use the blank spaces at the bottom of pages to record your responses to the questions asked.

On the last page of each chapter you will find "Make a Decision." Read this after you have completed the daily studies for the chapter. Determine to apply what you have learned during the week in your Bible study. *Develop the habit of searching the Scriptures for the solutions to life's problems.* The last pages of this book contain a list of books for further reading which will enrich your study as you refer to them.

It is also suggested that you use a notebook as you study, to record your further comments, questions and answers concerning the passages of Scripture you have read.

CHAPTER 1

God Created Man

"I believe in God the Father Almighty, maker of heaven and earth."

However, "no man hath seen God at any time." He is known by His works. "The heavens declare the glory of God; and the firmament showeth his handywork." One can look at the stars, the mountains, the seas, and see how great God is!

He is known by His functions, by what He does. He provides in His providence. He rules in His wisdom. He judges in His righteousness. He saves by His grace. He keeps by His faithfulness.

"All things were made by him; and without him was not anything made that was made"; He is the maker of all men.

Introductory Bible reading for this week: Genesis 1—10

1st Day　Genesis 1:1-10
God Created the Heaven and the Earth

God created all things and made everything I see. The Hebrew language uses two different verbs just as we do in English. "To create" in the Bible almost always means *to bring into existence out of nothing;* "to make" means *to produce a thing out of material already in hand.* A milliner can *create* a design for a woman's hat out of her own mind, conceiving a shape never seen before. Then she can take cloth and wire and beads and *make* the hat the woman can wear on her head. The verb "create," rarely used in Hebrew, is used more often in the first chapter of Genesis than in all the rest of the Old Testament. The verb "make" is a common word used ordinarily to indicate the production of anything. God is both creator and maker of all.

When the Bible says God created the heaven and the earth it means that He brought into existence the elements out of which He later "made" what we now see. When "created" the earth was "without form" and "empty." All was in "chaos"—we could say it was "raw material." But the elements now existed and could be used to "make" things of particular kinds—just as a tailor would have cloth out of which he could make coats, trousers, caps, and the like.

The first action God performed in making the elements into the world, which is the "cosmos" we know, was to say, "Let there be *light*." In chaos, "darkness" was everywhere. No one knows what light is. Our best description is that it is a form of energy in motion. Since light as energy comes from God, it seems very fitting that the name for God used at the beginning of the story of creation, means in the Hebrew language "The Strong One."

Where the light-energy moved was called "day." All the rest of creation which was not yet moving was called "night." This was the first distinction that appeared. Some part was moved by God, and the rest was still inert and empty.

To Go Further

Describe as many characteristics of "chaos" as you can.

How does taking any action change "chaos"?

What is necessary before action can be taken?

How do the opening verses of the Bible show the relation of God to the world?

2nd Day Genesis 1:11-19
God Created Plants

In creating plants God brought into existence things that could take elements into themselves to maintain their being what they were made to be. Such elements taken in thus are called "food." Plants were made to have a process of taking in food to maintain existence, and of giving off elements not needed. Thus plants must be in relationship with the environment so that the food needed may be available.

Plants also were made to have the capacity to reproduce their kind through seed. Plants produce fruit in which the seed appears which will reproduce other plants "after their kind."

All the chemical elements to be found in a plant came from the environment and were taken in as food. No research has been able to find any condition in the environment which will produce the growing process or the reproduction process. Although every plant uses the environment for growth and for reproduction, the trait that makes it a plant is not part of the environment. There is a profound truth in the saying, "only God can make a tree."

The process of growth and reproduction require certain conditions in the environment. Such were provided when God created the solar system and arranged the seasons. Sunlight is essential to plants, which were made with the capacity to derive from sunlight elements that are vital to growth and reproduction.

Although plants maintain existence by taking in elements from the environment, this is not automatic. There is an amazing selection of food in the vegetal process. The same field will sustain oak trees, apple trees and pumpkins.

At the same time there is an astonishing persistence in the kinds of plants that are reproduced. The phrase "after his kind" occurs three times in Genesis 1:11,12 emphasizing this persistent characteristic of "kind."

To Go Further

How much of the character of an oak tree is in the acorn?

How much of the oak tree depends on the environment?

What aspect of a tree can be seen as the result of natural process?

What aspects of a tree cannot be explained in terms of natural process?

What lessons can be learned to help understand how the Word of God is the "seed"?

3rd Day   Genesis 1:20-26
God Created Animals

In creating animals God brought into existence creatures that have all the traits of plants in their use of the environment as source of food for maintaining their existence and for propagating their kind, but they have more. Animals have locomotion. Just as plants are able to select food, so animals have capacity to select location. It may be that animals have some degree of self-consciousness. Certainly they have instincts of self-preservation and of self-fulfillment.

Animals are similar to plants in their reproduction process as indicated in the words "after his kind." In Genesis 1:20-25 this phrase is repeated seven times. This seems to emphasize in a special way that when animals reproduce it is their distinct characteristic that each progeny will be the same kind as the parent.

This special emphasis in the account of the creation of plants and animals is particularly significant in the light of modern popular speculation as to the origin of species. In this true and concise account of creation as recorded in Genesis 1:11,12 the phrase "after his kind" is used three times. Such repetition must carry weight in any candid reflection upon the record as given. It is clearly obvious that the Bible does not agree with any view that suggests any one kind of creatures would produce a different kind in later generations.

It is also amazing to note the order of creation which begins with plants and then follows with marine life, then birds and finally land animals with the vertebrate. This is the exact order proposed in modern zoology and biology. At the time of the writing of the Genesis account such sciences had not emerged. Nothing in the prevailing culture at that time would have suggested or supported the account as written in the Bible. Yet now the best thinking agrees with the biblical account. There is no problem in this for anybody who accepts the Genesis record as being the inspired truth.

To Go Further

What must one believe about God to accept Him as creator?

What must one believe about plants and animals to accept the Genesis record as true?

How important is it to believe Genesis 1 is true?

4th Day   Genesis 1:27-31
God Created Man

It has been said that the creation of man is the noblest work of God. The Bible tells the story of creation in such a way as to give the impression that the world was made to be the home of man.

"What is man, that thou art mindful of him? . . . For thou hast made him a little lower than the angels, . . . Thou madest him to have dominion over the works of thy hands; thou hast put all things under his feet" (Psalm 8:4-6).

Although the word "create" is used only rarely in the Hebrew Old Testament, it is used three times in the verse that tells about the creation of man (Genesis 1:27), emphasizing the importance of this particular act on the part of God.

The Hebrew word for "image" is the word for "shadow." Thus man was made "in the likeness" of God, as man's shadow would fall on the sand. The shadow on the sand would be only so much sand even though the man were flesh and blood. So in creation, man would be made of the dust of earth, but this would not be the essence of God.

It is probable that in his being a person, with thought, feeling and will, man is like God, who acts with cognition, emotion and volition. This may

7

show up mostly in man's capacity to know himself as a person, and in his ability to think and to plan creatively.

When man was told to subdue the earth and to have dominion over all creatures it would appear that he was the highest order in creation. Here is the implicit challenge for man to exercise all his capacity for scientific research and control to bring all creatures under his will.

In creation God acted in sovereign control, but in the course of man's life, man is to exercise his will in dominion over nature. What man does makes a difference.

To Go Further

How does his being "in the image of God" affect man's relation to the world?

How does man have dominion over nature?

How can man subdue the earth?

How did Jesus of Nazareth show His dominion over the processes of nature?

5th Day   Genesis 3:1-8
Man Sinned Against God

"Sin" is a "God-word." If the term "God" does not mean anything, "sin" does not mean anything. If "God" is great, "sin" is great! Sin is a want of conformity to, or a transgression of, the law of God. Sin

8

means anything that is not like God. No God means no sin.

When I accept the revelation in the Bible that God is the maker of heaven and earth, that He is my maker and my keeper and that He is my Judge, then I know that anything I am or do which is not according to His will is sin. Believing in God and confessing my sin are part of the same frame of mind.

To help me know His will, God has revealed the law and the gospel in the Bible. By the law is the knowledge of sin. When Adam was created the law had not been given, but God gave him a commandment to obey. The Word of God guided Adam into the way of blessing more effectually than any judgment of his own could have done.

When Adam trusted his own judgment and acted according to his own will, contrary to God's command he disobeyed God and thus sinned. God called him to account for what he had done and condemned him to die.

In grace God provided a way to escape death and to be reconciled to God.

To Go Further

At what point did the serpent begin the temptation?

Upon what considerations did Eve act in taking the forbidden fruit?

What truth is to be seen in the fact that the fruit was within the reach of Adam and Eve?

How was the responsibility of man to be seen?

What do you think you would have done, had you been in Adam's place?

6th Day   Genesis 3:9-24
God Judged Man

"The soul that sinneth, it shall die." This is the will of God revealed in the Bible. This fate is not so much imposed upon the sinner as a punishment, as it is implicit in the wrongdoing and comes as a consequence. This is not so much a threat of what God will do to the sinner because he disobeyed God's Word, as it is a warning of what will certainly follow because of the disobedient action of the wrongdoer.

In creating the world and man, God made things as He wanted them to be. Man was created in His image and was to be obedient to the Word of God. But man was also given a certain freedom of choice so that he could decide what he would do. However, he could not have any results he might wish. He could only have the results which would follow in the choices of conduct which he would make. Thus man had a certain freedom of choice which allowed him a freedom in action, but the results of his action could not be avoided.

God had definitely told Adam in His Word that he should not eat certain fruit, and warned him that if he disobeyed and ate the fruit, he would surely die. Satan tempted Adam to think that because the fruit was good for food, pleasant to look upon and would make one wise, it would be good to eat it.

In yielding to the temptation, Adam disobeyed the command of God and brought upon himself the consequence of death as he had been warned. In this world obeying the Word of God leads into life; disobeying the Word of God to follow one's own will leads into death.

To Go Further

Is being tempted a sin? (Compare Matthew 4:1 and Hebrews 4:15.)

At what point did Adam sin?

Why would the judgment of God be so important?

Why is the judgment of God unavoidable?

7th Day   Genesis 8:13-22
God Delivered Noah Through Grace

"The Lord knoweth how to deliver the godly out of temptations" (II Peter 2:9). In the Bible account of the judgment upon all men at the time of the Flood, the justice and the forbearance of God can be seen. But when the story of Noah and the ark is told, it is the grace of God that comes into view. There is no question but that the judgment was just and the plan to destroy the whole race quite proper. But the decision to spare Noah begins to show the grace of God.

11

In dealing with Noah God showed His interest in the individual. He will deal with each man according to that man's conduct. No man will ever be counted a sinner because his friends did wrong, and no man will ever be excused just because he associated with real believers.

God also showed His resourcefulness. The Flood would destroy all because it was a flood. But the ark would sail upon the flood. God's part was to show Noah how he could share in this deliverance.

God revealed the plan and the procedure. He described the ark and gave strength to Noah to build it. He then brought in the Flood. But He had made it possible for a believing man to escape the judgment by following the guidance revealed in His Word.

This profound truth is the basis of the gospel. Judgment by God is inevitable because of the sin of man. In judgment God will destroy unto death. But the ark enabled Noah and his family to escape the announced and actual judgment. Here it is obvious that even in judgment God remembers mercy and works to spare those who trust Him.

To Go Further

What does grace mean?

How does the story of the Flood show the general nature of judgment?

How does it show the special nature of grace?

Make a Decision

As we have completed our study of the creation of the world, the fall of man, and the wonderful provision of grace God has made for the repentant soul, has your heart been strangely warmed to praise God for His blessings of grace and mercy to the sons of men? If so, why not lift your heart in praise to God for what He has done, is doing and will do for all who turn to Him?

The one thing we can give to God is our praise and thanksgiving. Let's turn our hearts to God in praise and thanksgiving for all He has done for us in Christ Jesus. When we praise Him we open the door for more blessing.

CHAPTER 2

God Saves by Grace

The essence of the gospel is the amazing grace of God. "God commendeth his love toward us, in that, while we were yet sinners, Christ died for us" (Romans 5:8). For reasons of His own God created the world and made man a creature in His own image, with freedom of choice in action and responsibility in conduct. When man sinned he was judged and condemned to die. And yet—"Not by works of righteousness which we have done, but according to his mercy he saved us" (Titus 3:5).

God did the complete work of creation, and He does the complete work of salvation. In creation God took the dust of the earth and made man; in salvation God takes a sinner and makes him a child of God.

Introductory Bible reading for this week: Genesis 11—22

1st Day   Genesis 11:1-9
Man Cannot Save Himself

Salvation involves a radical change in the believer. This change cannot be effected by a person's own will power. It is so with the mind of a parent, which has certain distinctions that are not entirely the result of the parent's own intention or will. Children are necessary before the mind of a parent can develop. Even so, on another level, with salvation. Human efforts cannot save the soul.

Often when a person cannot do something in his own strength, he turns to others as though it could be done by joint effort. In many cases, this is a snare which deceives men. If a chain link is too weak to pull a load, the making of a longer chain out of twenty such weak links will not result in the strength that is needed. What one person weak in faith cannot do, twenty or a hundred persons just as weak cannot do. Multiplying weakness never produces strength.

The men of Babel tried to achieve a desirable goal by community effort. The Bible reveals that God appraised their intention as contrary to His will.

The clear testimony of human history is eloquent proof that unanimity in community efforts is beyond man's reach. Even Gamaliel could say with full confidence, "If this be of men, it will come to nought" (see Acts 5:38).

Salvation includes man's relationship with both God and man. In dealing with God certainly each man must turn to God in his own heart and receive

Jesus Christ as his own personal Saviour. In dealing with other men it will not be personal effort alone or community effort, but it will be "God which worketh in you both to will and to do of his good pleasure" (Philippians 2:13). It is "Christ in you, the hope of glory" (Colossians 1:27).

To Go Further

List all the community aspects in Genesis 11:1-9. List all aspects of dependence upon God in Genesis 12:1-4. List all aspects of dependence upon God in Hebrews 11:8-16.

2nd Day   Genesis 12:1-5
God Called Abraham

In creation God began making all men by making one. In salvation God began saving all who would be saved by saving one. Even in preparing a people whom He would use as an example of living by faith, God began by calling one man, Abraham. The Bible makes it clear that this is God's way of doing things. God deals with men one by one in bringing them to Himself.

No man takes it on himself to come to God. No man is good enough, strong enough, or wise enough to have fellowship with the Son of God, who perfectly does the will of His Father. But God in His grace calls men to Himself. He speaks His Word of promise to such as will respond in faith to obey Him.

God called Abraham to leave all that was his naturally, that he might come into a new situation, which would be given to him by God. He did not simply ask Abraham to change his way of living or to improve his personal conduct. He called on him to let go of all that he had that he might receive what God would give him.

Abraham did not know where he was going or what he would receive. His decision to obey was not based on any knowledge of what he would get, or on any comparison with what he had. Abraham believed and obeyed the Word of God.

Abraham was not chosen because he was better or stronger than anyone else. The Bible does not compare him to others. This teaches us that any person can come to God. It is both humbling and reassuring to know that we can come as we are. We are not counted as being particularly good and we are received, even if we are bad. "God is no respecter of persons."

To Go Further

What affect would it have on you if you thought God called only good people?

Compare the promise of God to Abraham (Genesis 12:1-3) with the goal of the men of Babel (Genesis 11:4). Contrast the procedure of Abraham with the procedure of the men of Babel. What lesson can I learn from the call of Abraham?

3rd Day   Genesis 13:5-13
Abraham Separated from Lot

The call of God includes guidance in daily affairs.
To believe in God means to obey His will. His guidance is not merely from place to place, but also in
matters of attitudes and personal relationships.
Walking in the will of God will affect my choice of
friends. If I follow the guidance of God I will separate from some of my former companions.

Lot was a nephew of Abraham, and a fellow believer in God. He had formerly lived in the same
country as Abraham and had come out of that land
in company with him.

Quarreling developed between the servants of
Lot and the servants of Abraham, and this was unacceptable to Abraham. He proposed to end the
strife by removing the rivalry over the land. He thus
set an example for all peacemakers by conceding
the grazing privileges to Lot and withdrawing to
another place.

Abraham made no attempt to define who was entitled to how much of the land. Nor did he propose
any restraints upon the servants of Lot. There is an
eloquent example here for all problems that involve
personal rights in social situations. Peace between
brethren is more important than priority or privilege (I Corinthians 6:7).

Obedience to the guidance of God led Abraham
in the way of peace. Fellowship with God was more
important to him than fellowship with his own kin.
Just as Abraham separated from his native land when
he set out to obey God, so he separated himself from

his fellow believer in continuing to obey God.

Separation was carried out at personal loss. When Abraham gave Lot the privilege to choose, he gave up his own claim to the best land.

To Go Further

On what grounds could Abraham have expected first choice of grazing land? What other procedure might have seemed proper to deal with the problem? Should Abraham have stayed on in fellowship with Lot? Is separation sometimes a natural development?

4th Day   Genesis 14:13-16
Abraham Rescued Lot

"Abraham believed God," and this became the source of the righteousness which was shown in his conduct. Believing God is not simply a mental exercise of accepting certain reports as accurate descriptions of events. It involves also yielding to God's will with an obedience that shapes conduct. James points out that Abraham believed God "when he had offered Isaac his son upon the altar." Likewise Rahab the harlot actually "believed" when she hid the spies. "Faith without works is dead," and Abraham's faith was most certainly not dead!

When Lot made his choice of land, he moved toward Sodom. In time he lived in that city. Abraham going in the opposite direction settled in the plains of Mamre ringed by mountains. When the kings of the plain captured Sodom, they took Lot and his household and carried them away as captives.

Abraham set an example for all godly men who have withdrawn from others in the interest of peace. Though separated from Lot in person, he nonetheless cared when he heard that Lot had been captured. He took steps at once to deliver him. By arming his own servants and leading them into battle he was able to defeat the kings and rescue Lot.

When the king of Sodom wanted to pay Abraham in gratitude for his release, Abraham refused to accept any of the spoils. He gave all the glory to God.

When Lot had been restored to his freedom Abraham returned to his place. He could work to rescue Lot, but that would not mean that he would share in his way of living. He would obey God and follow His guidance wherever it led.

To Go Further

What phrases in the narrative show Lot's progress into Sodom? Did Lot ever become like the men of Sodom (II Peter 2:7,8)? What lessons may church members of today learn from this story?

5th Day   Genesis 16:7-13
Ishmael Is Born of Hagar

Living by faith means that a person will follow the guidance of the Word of God. The believer will receive God's promises in dependence upon Him to do whatever is needed for their fulfillment. When God promised that his seed would be as the stars in number, Abraham counted upon that though at the time he had no son.

Sometimes, waiting upon God to fulfill His promise seems to take too long. When Abraham was old and Sarah was beyond the age when a woman would bear a child, they both thought the child would be born of Sarah's handmaid, Hagar. Abraham took her as his second wife and Ishmael was born.

Abraham loved Ishmael as his own son and apparently felt this would be a fulfillment of the promise of God. Sarah could not be satisfied, however, and dealt so harshly with Hagar that the handmaid fled. However, God halted Hagar in her flight, and bade her return to be obedient to Sarah.

Ishmael grew up as a child of trouble and strife. Yet Abraham loved him and taught him the truth of God. Some years after Isaac was born Abraham was commanded by God to send Ishmael away. This was a deep sorrow to Abraham, but his faith in God was so strong that he obeyed. In sending away Ishmael, Abraham again separated himself from his own.

The life of faith is not dependent upon human stratagems. The believer will face real temptation to do things apart from God's direction in order to bring God's promises to fulfillment, but this only leads to trouble.

If the believer would stop to think, he would realize that such rash procedure indicates awesome pride in his own wisdom and power but doubt as to God's.

To Go Further

Why did Sarah suggest that Abraham take Hagar as his second wife? Why did Sarah deal harshly with Hagar? What was unfortunate about the whole affair with Hagar?

6th Day   Genesis 21:1-8
Isaac Is Born of Sarah

"Sarah thy wife shall bear thee a son indeed; and thou shalt call his name Isaac" (Genesis 17:19). These words were spoken to Abraham when he was almost a hundred years old, and Sarah was ninety years old. The promise was ridiculous and Abraham laughed when he heard it. Later the promise was repeated to Abraham while seated in his tent door. When Sarah, standing behind the door, heard it she laughed at the impossibility of such an event.

But the messengers challenged both Abraham and Sarah to believe the promise of God. They did believe to the glory of God. Paul afterward commented about Abraham: "Being not weak in faith . . . he staggered not at the promise of God through unbelief . . . being fully persuaded that, what he had promised, he was able also to perform" (Romans 4:19-21). So Isaac was the child of promise.

Later in New Testament times, Paul made a point of the fact that Abraham had two sons: the first, Ishmael, was a child of the flesh, born in natural process; the second, Isaac, was a child of promise, born in the grace of God. The child of the flesh did not receive the promise.

Paul also pointed out that the child of the flesh came first and persecuted the child of the Spirit. He said this whole affair in Abraham's life was useful as an allegory to show spiritual truth (Galatians 4:22-31). Paul showed that Isaac was a symbol of all who are "born again," "born of the Spirit," the believers who are of the seed of Abraham because they believe in God.

Thus the Bible reveals the contrast of living in the flesh according to natural processes and living in the Spirit according to the promises of God. All who live by faith are "the seed of Abraham," and share in "the blessing of Abraham" (Galatians 3:7-14). This was fulfilled in the coming of the Holy Spirit, when God Himself came to dwell in the heart of the believer.

To Go Further

How is the experience of a Christian to be seen as the fulfillment of the promise to Abraham in Genesis 12:1-3? What spiritual truth may the Christian find in the story of Ishmael and Isaac? What parallel is to be seen in the births of Isaac and Jesus, and what does this teach us about salvation?

7th Day   Genesis 22:6-13
Abraham Offers Up Isaac

"By faith Abraham, when he was tried, offered up Isaac" (Hebrews 11:17-19). The greatest demonstration of faith in the life of Abraham was the offering up of Isaac. The fulfillment of the promise that he should have an innumerable seed was centered in this child of promise: "In Isaac shall thy seed be called." Offering up Isaac meant that Abraham was committing to God the eventual fulfillment of the promise.

The book of Hebrews comments that Abraham did this "by faith," counting that God was able to raise him from the dead, "from whence also he received him in a figure." Abraham's faith was not in his own action, as though he were earning a reward, but in God. He would put no limit on what God could do. If now God wanted Abraham to offer up Isaac unto death, he would not question God.

There is much to be learned here about living by faith. The believer accepts the will of God as set forth in His Word. He expects the fulfillment of the promises as these are given. The believer simply trusts God to keep His Word.

The believer does not watch the processes of nature at work to gain confidence in God. Assuredly God is creator and sustainer. But more wonderful still—He is redeemer, the God of all grace and the keeper of all His gracious promises.

To Go Further

What does this incident show about Abraham's love of his son? What does it show of Isaac's obedience to his father? List the several successive crises in Abraham's career involving separation from his loved ones.

Make a Decision

Living by faith is a life of separation. We are separated from sin, but we are also called to be "separated unto the gospel of God" (Romans 1:1). That is, we are not our own; we are now to be set aside for "God's use only." This is the way of victory and joyful service unto God.

Abraham realized this blessing in his personal life. But it cost him everything. The cost is still the same, but so is the blessing. It can be yours for the same price: all of you—your material goods, your family, and lastly yourself. The price is great, but not nearly so great as the blessing to follow.

CHAPTER 3

God Keeps His Word

The covenant with Abraham included the promise of blessing. God gave assurance that He would keep Abraham, give him victory over his enemies, and give him a seed that would be as numerous as the stars, and a land in which to dwell. None of this was based on Abraham's performance since it was all promised before Abraham had begun living by faith.

The promise was to be the pattern of God's dealing with Isaac, with Jacob, and then with Joseph. The Bible shows that God was faithful to His promise in the lives of the patriarchs. The blessing continued to be given to each generation as promised to Abraham.

Introductory Bible reading for this week: Genesis 23–50

1st Day   Genesis 25:27-34
Jacob Secures the Birthright

Jacob was the younger twin. In the custom of the day the firstborn had certain privileges and benefits apart from any action on his own part. One of the advantages of being firstborn was to receive the major share of whatever legacy was left by the father. As Isaac had inherited the promise of God in the covenant, so his oldest son Esau was entitled to inherit this blessing as his birthright. Jacob knew about this promise and greatly esteemed its worth. He longed to have the birthright which Esau would naturally inherit.

Jacob was hungry at the end of his day of working in the fields. He prepared himself a meal, which was ready to be eaten when Esau came in hungry after a day of hunting. Esau wanted the meal Jacob had prepared for himself, and was willing to exchange his birthright for this food. Though Jacob wanted the meal, he esteemed the birthright so important that he was willing to deny himself in order to secure it.

"Jacob have I loved, but Esau have I hated" (Romans 9:13). This statement can be understood in the light of this incident about the birthright. Paul used this Scripture to emphasize the foreknowledge of God; before the twins had done anything, God in His foreknowledge knew how each would respond to his hunger.

Some actions a man takes are final. When a man cuts down a sapling two feet tall he has settled forever that the plant will never be an oak tree. When

Esau sold his birthright for a mess of pottage he settled forever that he would never have that blessing.

Jacob denied himself food when he was hungry that he might receive the blessing of God. Later, Jesus of Nazareth refused to turn stones into bread because obedience to His Father was more important than food for His physical body. This is the basic principle of spiritual living.

To Go Further

Name some common temptations which can lure a Christian to choose the natural way of living.

Show how denying self would be the answer to various modern situations.

How would denying yourself and yielding to Christ in certain so-called minor matters affect your domestic situation?

2nd Day   Genesis 26:12-19
Isaac Is Blessed

Blessing from God was a major part of the covenant with Abraham. "I will bless thee." God will bless according to His own will, but such blessing is not arbitrary. The believer must ordinarily respond in obedience to the revealed will of God in order to receive the blessing.

The blessing of God is not some one specific benefit given as a bonus or reward for obedience. The form of blessing will be related to the particular situation. "Then Isaac sowed in that land, and received in the same year an hundredfold: and the Lord blessed him" (Genesis 26:12). Here the blessing upon the sowing was a good crop with a heavy yield. In Genesis 26:19 we read, "Isaac's servants digged in the valley, and found there a well of springing water." Here the action was digging in a certain spot, and the blessing was "a well of springing water."

This truth is very important for an understanding of the life of faith. God blesses action taken in obedient response to His guidance. Isaac would never have been blessed with a large yield if he had not sown the seed. It is impossible to guide the journey of a man who is sitting in a rocking chair on the porch. There is something obviously lacking when one prays for faith but does not read and study the Bible. "Faith cometh by hearing, and hearing by the word of God." To neglect the Bible and then to pray for faith is not the way of faith.

In blessing, God usually adds to whatever is being done. "I have planted, Apollos watered; but God gave the increase" (I Corinthians 3:6). This seems to emphasize the primary importance of obedience. The promise, "I will bless thee," seems to stand unconditionally as the sovereign purpose of God—but these words appear in a context. The Word of God began with a call, "Get thee out of thy country, and from thy kindred, and from thy father's house, unto a land that I will show thee" (Genesis 12:1). The promise of blessing followed. It was because Abraham obeyed and went out "not knowing whither he went" that the blessing came upon him.

To Go Further

Note the several times when Abraham first obeyed and then was blessed. If I wanted blessing of a certain sort, and I believed in God, what should I do?

3rd Day   Genesis 27:22-29
Jacob Secures the Blessing of Isaac

The blessing of God promised to Abraham was also promised to his seed. God had told Abraham "thou shalt be a blessing" (Genesis 12:2). Later the Word was more specific, "And in thy seed shall all the nations of the earth be blessed" (Genesis 22:18). In some way obscure to our understanding Isaac had the capacity to invoke this blessing upon Jacob "and give thee the blessing of Abraham, to thee, and to thy seed with thee."

The promise of God's blessing was very important in the eyes of Jacob. He worked with his mother Rebekah to deceive his nearly blind father and presented himself to Isaac as Esau. Isaac thus gave Jacob the blessing by mistake.

Much of this incident is puzzling to the reader. Before they were born, the mother was told that "the elder shall serve the younger" (Genesis 25:23).

As young men, Jacob secured the birthright from Esau when Esau wanted to eat his meal. Was there any real need that Rebekah and Jacob should plan to deceive Isaac?

The incident reveals an important truth. Even though Jacob's conduct was not above reproach, yet he received the favor of God. It seems quite clear that God blesses the believer not simply as a reward for virtue. If Jacob were to have received what he deserved he would never have been blessed of God. But he did highly esteem the favor of God, and he would give up what he had to get that blessing. Even though a man may not act as he should, he can yet have a profound faith in God and a deep desire for blessing. This may incline him to look to God for favor and to yield himself to the will of God, as revealed in His Word. It is to the glory of God that Christ receiveth sinful men.

To Go Further

List the actions of Jacob that we would consider wrong. What did Jacob ever do that could bring him into blessing? What lessons can we learn here for our living by faith?

4th Day   Genesis 28:10-22
God Appears to Jacob at Bethel

Faith in God can be grounded in what we learn from others. Jacob was one of the children of Isaac and so shared in all the traditions of the family. Certainly Isaac and Rebekah would teach their children about God and the promises to Abraham.

A knowledge of God can be transformed into loving trust when the individual is brought into personal confrontation with the living God. The family life of Isaac and Rebekah would have inclined Jacob to believe in God, but when God appeared to him in a dream at Bethel, he received convictions that affected the course of his life.

Like any dream, no one else had it or knew it. In the dream God spoke to Jacob personally. God identified Himself as the God of Abraham and the God of Isaac, and made it clear He would now be the God of Jacob. When Jacob saw the stairway leading from earth to heaven, he could understand that heaven was as real as the earth, and that they were connected with each other. When he saw angels ascending and descending he understood that what happened in one mattered in the other.

When he heard the voice of the Lord uttering to him the promise of Abraham, Jacob knew God would bless him forever.

When Jacob awoke from his sleep he was aware that he was in the very presence of God. He was deeply awed by this truth, and immediately committed himself to worship and to serve God.

To Go Further

Would you say that this story indicated Jacob was bargaining with God to gain His favor?

Why is it important for a person to know the history of God's dealings with His people?

What can you do to retain the consciousness of the presence of God?

5th Day Genesis 32:24-32
God Appears to Jacob at Peniel

Living by faith depends upon strong convictions about God. Convictions about God can grow deeper and stronger. Convictions can be grounded in the testimony of others, especially of one's own family (II Timothy 3:14,15). They can be confirmed and developed in personal experience. They can grow by repeated personal confrontations with God. God had appeared to Jacob at Bethel and again while he was serving Laban. But the climax of his dealing with God occurred at Peniel (Genesis 32:24-32).

After serving Laban for twenty years, Jacob decided to return to Canaan. While on the way, he heard that his estranged brother Esau was coming out to meet him with four hundred men. Esau had vowed to kill him before he left home.

First, Jacob planned certain procedures to escape total annihilation at the hands of an angry Esau. But he did not have full confidence in all he had done. When he had done all he could in his own wisdom, Jacob turned to God for help.

The classic struggle in wrestling with the messenger all night long revealed the persistence of Jacob's trust in God.

After much struggling the messenger crippled Jacob by rendering one leg useless. But Jacob still would not let go. When day was breaking the messenger told Jacob that his persistence had prevailed. Jacob's name was changed to Israel, to show that he had conducted himself as a "prince with God."

The next day his meeting with Esau was peaceful and cordial. Esau offered to include Jacob in his company. But Jacob wisely excused himself and went on alone. It is important to note that even in praying there is no sense in which a believer "earns" the blessing, or even is "worthy." What God does for sinners, He does in His grace.

To Go Further

Did Jacob have any reason to expect God to bless him with protection?

Even if a believer has the promise of God, is there anything for him to do to get the blessing?

How does the experience of Jacob seem like an example of every man as he looks to his own past?

6th Day   Genesis 37:23-28
Joseph Is Sold into Slavery

Living by faith may lead the believer into real trouble. He is often vulnerable to ill treatment by other men. Decisions are made and action is taken along the line of the revealed will of God. This is not always acceptable to others. When obedience brings blessing to the believer, other men are filled with envy. They may become malicious. Then the believer encounters trouble he did not cause and did not expect. And such trouble can be very real.

Joseph grew up as the beloved son of his father. His own disposition was to be honest and trustworthy. He was faithful to his task when he was sent to bring a report of the activities of his brothers, and told his father the truth. His jealous brothers were very resentful and sold him as a slave to strangers, who took him to Egypt.

As a slave, he was so competent and reliable that Potiphar entrusted all he had to Joseph's care. Because he refused to be seduced from his integrity, Potiphar's wife slandered Joseph, who was then cast into prison.

As a prisoner, he was so trustworthy that the warden put him in charge of all the prisoners. Although he was promised redress, he was forgotten and remained in prison.

In time he had the opportunity to show his ability before Pharaoh, who at once took him out of prison and put him in charge of governing of the whole nation.

In all these misfortunes, caused by evil persons who were hostile because of envy and jealousy, Joseph did not lose his confidence in God nor did he apparently develop a bitter spirit toward his persecutors. The grace of God enabled him to keep in mind the overruling providence of God.

When his brothers feared that he would take steps to retaliate for the ill treatment he received, he quickly put their minds at rest. He explained that he had accepted all that happened as being God's will and had full confidence that all would work together for good. This is a truly classic example of confidence in the providence of God.

To Go Further

Did Joseph do wrong when he told his father how his brothers were acting in their work?

Was it wrong for Joseph to tell his brothers about his dreams?

In what way was the life of Joseph like that of Jesus?

7th Day   Genesis 41:38-44
Joseph Becomes the Ruler

Living by faith can bring the believer into places of service far beyond any expectation or intention of his own. God always does more than one can ask or think. To live in obedience to the will of God can lead the believer into places of opportunity he would never have reached in his own efforts. The believer can handle such opportunities better because he is so much aware that it is God who is opening the way and making gracious provision for needs.

Joseph as a boy had dreams in which he saw himself in a place of leadership and honor above his brethren, but he had no idea that one day a whole nation would bow to his authority. "Thou hast been faithful over a few things, I will make thee ruler over many things" (Matthew 25:21). By being obedient in the lesser he was brought into the greater.

In Joseph's case the situation was one of service and authority. Joseph did not reach the prominent or important place because of his own ability or his great knowledge. His life was under the control of God.

In living in obedience to God, Joseph came to the place where he could give real help to his father and to his brothers. By obeying the will of God he was led into situations far greater than he could ever have reached by himself.

To Go Further

How did Joseph's earlier experiences fit him for the great work he was to do later?

Did Joseph's personal attitude affect his opportunity for advancement in his work?

What foremost lesson can you learn from the career of Joseph?

Make a Decision

God has promised great and glorious blessings to those who put their trust in Him. God always keeps

His Word, so we can always claim each promise with assurance that it will come to pass just as He said.

Sometimes in the providence of God one must wait for the promised blessing, but it always comes at God's appointed time. Are you waiting for a specific blessing from the Lord? Don't give up; He hasn't forgotten. God has promised that we shall reap if we faint not. God's time is always "just right." Always the word comes to us: "Wait on the Lord . . . wait, I say, on the Lord."

CHAPTER 4

God Saves His People

The gospel of Jesus Christ offers salvation to "whosoever will come" in response to the call of God. "He that believeth on me hath everlasting life" (John 6:47). Those who respond to the call are the people of God.

God will save His people. He will pardon their iniquities, He will forgive their sins, He will redeem their souls, He will deliver them from evil, He will sustain them in strength, He will guide them by His will, He will comfort them by His Spirit, He will bring them to Himself and He will keep them forever. This is His work. Man cannot do any part of this in his own wisdom and strength. Christ is the "one mediator between God and men" (I Timothy 2:5).

Introductory Bible reading for this week: Exodus 1—12; 14;15

1st Day   Exodus 1:8-14
Israel Is Enslaved in Egypt

The Bible tells the story of how God will bless His people in His grace and by His power. In His wisdom God created the world in such a way that we fulfill His commands only when we overcome the world, even at the cost of suffering pain and distress. To show how this plan works, God used Israel as an example.

Although the land of Canaan was promised to Abraham to be his possession and the inheritance of his seed, the children of Israel did not begin their history as citizens in that land. Rather, they were strangers in Egypt where they aroused envy and fear so that they were persecuted and enslaved by the Egyptians.

Though God is gracious and kind, and though He had promised to bless Abraham's seed, He allowed the Egyptians to enslave and to abuse His people. Despite their suffering the children of Israel were not ready to leave Egypt, but it would be necessary in obeying the will of God for them to leave their home and journey to a new and strange land. The harsh treatment by the Egyptians made them willing to go.

Any human being is first born into this world as a natural man. When the gospel is presented to him there is a call that requires him to turn away from the natural, from this world, that he might receive the spiritual, the eternal life of God. But man can become attached to the natural world. God will not force him to turn, but will call him to turn to Him.

God will offer him life in place of death, joy instead
of sorrow, assurance rather than fear. Man must decide to choose the promise of God. Often it is only
after he suffers distress in this world that a man will
turn to God.

To Go Further

What are some of the sorrows in this life that
make a person willing to turn to God? Can you see
why God allows some believers to suffer severe
hardship? What are some of the things which could
happen to a young person to make him willing to
turn to God?

2nd Day   Exodus 4:18-23
Moses Is Raised Up to Deliver Israel

The life of faith is based on the believer's obedience in response to the call of God. God's Word offers a promise to man of what God will do for anybody, whosoever will come unto Him. This promise
needs to be uttered to man in a way that he can understand, so that he can respond in obedience. So
that man would be able to believe the promise and
hear the call, God in His grace would send messengers, prophets, who would speak the message to
man. The greatest prophet was Christ Jesus the
Lord.

When God used Israel to demonstrate how He would lead His people, God sent His servant Moses to the children of Israel to call them into His will. God did not send an angel, like Gabriel, to communicate His promise to Israel, but He raised up one of themselves, Moses, of the tribe of Levi.

Since Moses was a Hebrew just as the other children of Israel, he could more easily win their confidence and also contribute to their understanding. When he called them to obey the will of God, he was among them as a man, like themselves, and could lead them into obedience because he would know in himself what was involved for them.

Because he was only a man, he was in danger of what they might do to him. But this would be all the more reason why they could see what it meant to obey God. If it seemed dangerous to obey God, Moses himself faced that danger. This gave his message greater acceptance by the people.

The Israelites could be delivered only if they would obey the call of God, as given to them by Moses. When they could understand him, because he was one of them, they were able to understand the will of God. And this enabled them to obey intelligently—they could do His will and know what they were doing.

To Go Further

How does the career of Moses compare with the career of Jesus of Nazareth? Why did Christ take on human form? What help is it for a sinner to realize that Jesus of Nazareth was tempted as we are?

3rd Day   Exodus 5:6-13
Pharaoh Oppresses Israel

The distress and hardship endured in this world by the people of God as they move to obey Him are sometimes caused by stubborn opposition on the part of the settled powers of the status quo. All men find their place in their social setting and others would prefer that no one begins any move to change the established situation in which each is assigned his place and role. Any attempt to change the established situation is often regarded a threat to personal security and thus is resisted.

In Egypt the Hebrews were aliens, but more—in a vain attempt to reduce their number, the Egyptians had put them in bondage as slaves. Despite their harsh persecution the Hebrews multiplied. In time their distress became so great that the people cried unto God for relief.

When Moses requested permission for the children of Israel to go three days' journey into the wilderness that they might worship God, Pharaoh took a determined stand against such permission. He accused the people of being idle, and proceeded to increase the burdens already imposed upon them.

Moses performed certain miracles to demonstrate to Pharaoh his authentic status as a leader sent from God. When his magicians performed similar miracles, Pharaoh hardened his heart in firm refusal to grant permission. When Moses brought more plagues to harass the Egyptians, the magicians were convinced he was from God and advised Pharaoh to grant the permission requested. But Pharaoh continued in his obdurate stand until more plagues brought greater distress upon his people.

Pharaoh was reluctant to allow Israel to leave and proposed four successive compromises to Moses' request. But Moses was firm in his stand, refusing to accept any compromise.

To Go Further

What "status quo circumstances" are changed when a man accepts Christ? Who would have any interest in opposing the winning of souls to Christ? What lessons can be learned from the way Moses handled the offers to compromise?

4th Day   Exodus 8:15-19
Moses Brings Plagues upon Egypt

"God is the ruler yet." The truth about God and the world is that God is on the throne. God's sovereignty, however, does not mean that He coerces all His creatures to obey Him. He calls men to Himself and guides the willing ones by His will into blessing. Some will be unwilling and disobedient. While

God does not lead those by His Word, He is nevertheless in control of such factors as will bring them, even though unwillingly, into His purposes. But when this is done in this way there is no blessing for the disobedient.

Israel needed the permission of Pharaoh to come out of Egypt. Pharaoh refused to grant permission, but persecuted the Hebrews even more harshly than before. God then instructed Moses to bring plagues upon Egypt, one after another.

Certain magicians in Pharaoh's court produced wonders similar to the first plagues. This influenced Pharaoh to harden his heart in refusal to grant the request of Moses.

As the plagues became more grievous, Pharoah offered several compromises. Moses rejected each offer. The plagues became worse and worse. Pharaoh gave in for a while. Moses had the people prepared, and they promptly departed when Pharaoh gave permission.

Troubles in the world are after all under the mighty hand of God. Some people do not take the issues of God's will and God's blessing to heart until they suffer much. Not all suffering may be related to spiritual living, but much of it is.

In the case of Israel in Egypt, God brought the plagues to distress Egypt so that His people would gain permission to leave the country. The plagues did not really change Pharaoh's heart or spirit. As soon as the shock of the loss of the firstborn was over, Pharaoh pursued the children of Israel to force them to return. The world persists in its evil intention to oppose the things of God.

To Go Further

What did the plagues show Israel? What did the plagues teach Pharaoh?

What are some conditions today that incline the community to tolerate an active church?

5th Day   Exodus 10:20-26
Pharaoh Tries to Compromise

When Pharaoh began to feel that the plagues were unbearable he tried to compromise with Moses. This is a very important revelation of a situation the people of God must face. The opposition of Pharaoh is the opposition of the natural world today, which is offended when Christians want to live their lives separated from the world. And today the world offers to the Christians compromises which threaten to hinder spiritual victory.

Pharaoh first offered to allow Israel to worship God "in the land" (Exodus 8:25). Moses pointed out this would not be acceptable.

Then Pharaoh proposed that they "not go very far away" (Exodus 8:28). But Moses refused this.

After more plagues, Pharaoh proposed that the adult Hebrews should go, but leave the children (Exodus 10:8-11). Again Moses rejected the proposal.

Finally Pharaoh agreed to everyone going, old and young, but he proposed they should "let your flocks and your herds be stayed" (Exodus 10:24). Once again Moses refused to compromise.

In these four proposals are to be seen clear descriptions of compromises that face believers to this day. When the people of God want to worship God, they feel they want to withdraw to be by themselves. The people of the world do not want this.

Even when Christians feel they must make some difference in their conduct, the people of the world want these differences to be as little as possible: "not go very far away."

When the believers insist they must be entirely different, then the people of the world ask them not to insist on their children coming along.

When Christians insist their children must come with them, then the world suggests there should be no change in conduct of practical affairs. After all, "business is business."

To Go Further

Why would the world want Christians to act just as non-Christians? Why would the world want Christians to let their children do as other children do? How do you as a Christian personally respond to these wants?

6th Day   Exodus 12:29-39
The Passover

When Moses announced the final plague in which the firstborn would die throughout the land, he instructed the children of Israel as to how they could escape the plague. The angel of death would go through the whole land, and every firstborn was under sentence of death. But there was a procedure anyone could follow by which the firstborn would be spared.

The household that wanted to escape the judgment was to sacrifice a lamb, sprinkling the blood upon the doorposts. The promise was "when I see the blood, I will pass over you." This became one of the major elements in the faith of Israel. This idea was so significant that Moses made of it an annual feast.

Certain lessons were clearly taught in this whole event. The individual Hebrew would slay his lamb as instructed, if he believed, and he would be spared. Any who did not obey the instructions through unbelief would suffer death, as the Lord had said. The procedure was given by God to all, but it was forced on no one. Those who believed and obeyed were spared.

Apparently there was no judgment upon the character or record of the believer. God looked upon the blood on the doorpost. He passed over to spare the family because of the blood.

Also there was no attention given to the state of mind of those in the house. If the blood was there the family was spared, no matter how they felt.

Jesus of Nazareth was called "the Lamb of God." This indicated that He would die so that anyone believing in Him might live and have eternal life. His death on Calvary was the shedding of the blood which atones for the sins of the believer. When God sees the death of Jesus Christ on my behalf, and sees that I am trusting in Him, He will "pass over" me and I will become one of His people.

To Go Further

How was faith shown by the putting of blood on the doorposts?

Would the Hebrew with a particularly high ethic be any safer than any other who put the blood on the door?

Why would anyone not put the blood on the door?

7th Day   Exodus 14:26-31
Pharaoh Is Destroyed

Our response to the Word of God is a matter of life and death. Every man is a sinner and is doomed to death. The grace of God is greater than all our sin, and He has provided a salvation which can be had by anyone who will heed His call and come to Him. Eternal life is offered to all who will come. But men hesitate to come because in coming they must confess their sin and inability to overcome it, deny themselves, and accept what God provides.

Man by nature is in himself sinfully selfish. The things of this world fascinate him, and he does not want to give them up.

When God calls a man to Himself that he might

be saved, God calls him out of this world, out of his kindred, and even out of himself. He must be willing to forsake all, that he might accept what God offers to him in the gospel.

This truth is demonstrated in the history of Israel. The children of Israel had lived in Egypt for over 400 years, but this was not their home. The promise of blessing given to Abraham included their living in the promised land of Canaan.

The conflict between Moses and Pharaoh was finally ended when Israel crossed the Red Sea to be free from the power of Egypt. In the course of that significant event, Pharaoh was destroyed.

There is an important lesson here for every believer. In the very event of his being born again and given newness of life, all the natural elements that held him in bondage are destroyed. The Christian can really be delivered "from this present evil world" by accepting the salvation in Christ.

To Go Further

How is the death and resurrection of Jesus Christ like the crossing of the Red Sea?

How is the crossing of the Red Sea like the beginning of "the newness of life"?

How is a believer set free from this world?

Make a Decision

The Christian often finds himself in a situation which calls for a definite action. In all circumstances the Christian can turn to God for help and guidance. To the praise of God and the salvation of the believer, God will hear the call and will come to the believer's deliverance. At such times God not only shows the Christian the way, but also works out the arrangements for the opening up of the way before him. Do you need help from the Lord in your present situation? If so, it is available. God is only a prayer away.

CHAPTER 5

God Guides His People

Living in the will of God is traveling through the unknown under His guidance. No man knows what a day will bring forth. And no one knows what lies ahead at the next turn of the road. But God knows and can guide His people in His wisdom to their benefit.

No doubt God in His power could have made the world so that His people would automatically do His will, but this He did not do. He made man in a way that left him a certain freedom of choice. He planned that man should be blessed as he would obey the will of God, but man should obey because it was his choice. Thus he would freely walk in the way that God would lead him.

Introductory Bible reading for this week: Exodus 13; 16—24

1st Day   Exodus 13:17-22
By Cloud and Fire

The blessing of God as promised to Abraham in the covenant included the presence of God with his people. It would be of the utmost importance for them to choose the right way. Since God knew what lay ahead at any time, He could guide them for their good and for His glory.

The guidance of God was given in the daytime by a cloud, and at night by a pillar of fire. The cloud would guide, not by moving ahead of the children of Israel so that they would follow it where they saw it go, but by serving as a shade in the heat of the sun. When the cloud moved, they moved along to stay in its shadow.

At nighttime they were led by the pillar of fire. With darkness all around, the light from the pillar of fire was a distinct practical advantage. By staying in the light they would see where to avoid pitfalls and how to find the smooth road.

In all this a profound truth is shown to all who follow the Lord. There can be immediate circumstances that appeal because of their promise of practical benefit. But these may also be very significant because following their guidance may result in permanent blessing far beyond the range of the immediate situation. But all of this is under the guidance of the Lord, who is bringing His people along His way according to His own will.

God's people may respond to the obvious benefits of certain conduct with only the immediate practical advantage in mind. It would belong to the wisdom and the power of God that the ultimate and spiritual benefits would be served in the very course chosen and taken by His people, even though unknown to the people making the decisions.

To Go Further

Describe a situation in which persons might choose for immediate benefit, a course of action which could have eternal benefits. What can be learned in this about God's way of leading His people? Illustrate this principle by one of your own experiences.

2nd Day Exodus 16:14-21
Nourished by Bread from Heaven

Living by faith involves a daily dependence upon the Lord. Not only is the believer guided directly by the will of God, but he is nourished directly from the Lord. The natural man maintains his existence by and derives his strength from his use of his physical environment. His body lives by the bread which he eats. The spiritual man maintains his spiritual existence by and derives his spiritual strength from his use of the Word.

This was illustrated in the case of Israel as the people of God launched out from Egypt to cross the desert and to enter into the land of Canaan, depending upon God. Upon leaving Egypt they took bread dough with them to ensure their food supply. But in time this provision was gone.

Moses turned to God in his extremity. All were amazed at the appearance of the manna which appeared on the ground each morning, six days every week.

Certain conditions prevailed about its use. It had to be gathered before sunrise, because in the heat of the day it would disappear. It was not to be gathered on the Sabbath day. On the day before the Sabbath, each man would gather enough for two days and it would keep without spoiling. If any man gathered an oversupply in hoarding fashion on any other day, it would spoil in his storehouse.

By this means Israel was reminded how dependent upon God they were. The humble could rejoice that their neeeds were being met. They could realize nothing depended ultimately on their wit or strength. They could also see that their obedience was directly the basis of their blessing.

To Go Further

In what ways was the manna similar to the Word of God to the believer today?

What lessons are to be learned from the regulations which governed the collecting of the manna?

In your own structure of values, how does your daily bread compare with your daily devotions?

Of the two, which are you more likely to skip in an emergency?

3rd Day   Exodus 17:1-7
Refreshed by Water from the Rock

Living by faith is not only possible but is actually much more effectual than living solely in dependence upon natural processes. All living is possible only by use of the environment. In natural living, food and drink are found as natural elements in the natural environment, but in living by faith food and drink are provided from God Himself.

The Christian has both of these processes in his own experience. Every Christian begins his life as a natural human being with a physical body which needs physical food and physical drink to stay alive. When he is born again by the grace of God through the Word of God, he is a new creature. He now has in him eternal life which needs the Word of God, as food and drink, that he might live as a child of God in Jesus Christ.

The natural man receives his necessary food and drink from the natural physical environment. Man needs to discriminate in what he will take as food and drink. The world in which man was created and where he lives, contains elements both good and bad, both vital and fatal. There is both food and poison within his reach.

The spiritual man receives his necessary food and drink from the Word of God. Here also man must take heed as to what he hears. Man needs to discriminate as to what he will accept as the true Word of God. There are many voices to be heard, and some would deceive—even as the serpent deceived Eve. Error when believed can lead to death.

What is brought to the believer in the Word is from God. Even as the manna from heaven and the water from the rock, the Word of God is not a natural product. There is something original and spontaneous as creation in the revelation of God's will to His people. "Flesh and blood" cannot reveal it to the soul. Neither reason nor logic can discover it. Apparently God has reserved His creative prerogative to Himself and will not give His glory to another.

To Go Further

How may the Christian discriminate between truth and error in the preaching he hears?

Explain the difference between theology and philosophy. What response do you expect on the part of natural man to the message of the Bible?

4th Day   Exodus 17:8-13
United Intercession Brings Victory

Living by faith brings the power of God to the help of the believer. But this help is often not given apart from the exercise of believing on the part of the people of God. Even when there is a general promise of help, such help will often not materialize in a certain situation apart from specific faith in that particular case. This faith can be exercised in prayer and can result in definite answers that will affect the outcome of the specific situation.

Moses was leading Israel across the desert in the assurance that God was with them, helping their progress day by day. Each morning the manna fell to remind them of God's faithful provision. The cloud by day and the pillar of fire by night were constant evidences of God's guidance.

But when Amalek attacked Israel, and Moses sent Joshua to battle against him, a new situation arose that required help from God. In open battle with Amalek, Joshua was being defeated.

But now a new dimension of need was seen. Although Moses' praying was able to bring the help of God to enable Joshua to prevail, the limitation of Moses' own weakness threatened to allow Joshua to come to defeat. At this point two relatively lesser men, Aaron and Hur, came to help Moses to pray, and this turned the tide of battle.

The great lesson is not only an emphasis upon the effectiveness of intercessory prayer but that united intercessory prayer is supremely effective. Certainly Joshua's military effort was essential and the praying of Moses was the key to victory, but it was the united help of Aaron and Hur that enabled Moses to continue in intercessory prayer until the crisis was past and the victory was won.

To Go Further

What is the challenge to all believers in this incident? What benefits for believers as a whole can be seen in this account? How can any congregation profit by the lessons in this event?

5th Day   Exodus 18:14-23
Moses Helped by Organization

Living in faith includes the possibility that the believer may be led into activity where the immediate demands require more than he can personally do. In such a case the believer can be helped by others.

It is true that each believer enters as an individual into personal, private relations and dealings with God. But the individual lives in a group and serves God as he deals with the other members of his group. The believer is still an individual and the issues of life and service are settled between himself and God, but in living his life he is involved with others.

As the children of Israel began living under the guidance of the Ten Words, they often encountered situations that were obscure to their understanding. For a time each person would come to Moses for his advice and help. But there were so many cases that Moses was actually swamped with overwork.

Jethro, Moses' father-in-law, helped by giving Moses some sound practical advice. The accumulation of cases waiting for Moses' personal attention could be relieved if certain capable men were given some of Moses' authority and asked to act in the place of Moses. This system of helpers worked out well because: (1) it brought into function more leaders, (2) it gave the people a sense of their participation which ensured their interest, (3) it humbled Moses to realize he was not the only servant of God.

Sometimes it will be said that to be spiritual and from the Lord, leadership should be spontaneous without any planning or structure. This is not what the Bible teaches about the ways of God. More can be done with less cost by arranging to have the "common" people do their part along the way.

To Go Further

How would delegating responsibility to fellow workers affect Moses? How would it affect the fellow workers? How does this incident illustrate what could be done in a Sunday School?

6th Day   Exodus 20:18-26
The Ten Words Reveal God's Will

Living by faith involves working along lines that are in the will of God. The will of God is eternal and determines what is right and what is wrong. Thus these concepts are much older than creation itself. God's judgment is part of His eternal will. There never was any time when anything else would have been acceptable. The will of God is part of God Himself and so is eternal.

But the will of God is invisible. No man by searching can find out God, and no man by any sort of reasoning can find out the will of God. But God can reveal Himself, and God can reveal His will.

When Moses went to the top of Mount Sinai to meet with God, he was given the two tablets of stone on which had been written the Ten Words "with the finger of God." The Ten Words, which were later to be called the Ten Commandments, are known in Scripture as "the Law of Moses" and "the Law of God." They spell out in human words what the nature of God demands of His creatures.

The Ten Words can be grouped into two sections. The first four refer to man's relationship with God, the last five to man's relationship with man. The fifth can be included in either group. In a very real sense parents function in the place of God toward their children. When children honor their parents they are actually honoring God. On the other hand, when children honor their parents they are acting righteously toward men.

It is important to remember that the Ten Words were given to Moses to help in guiding a redeemed, delivered, committed people into the blessing of God in their daily affairs.

To Go Further

How do the first and second great commandments (Matthew 22:36-40) compare with the Ten Words?

In what way can the Ten Words be used as a means of coming to God? What application do the Ten Words have to us who live on this side of the Cross?

7th Day   Exodus 24:1-8
Moses Explained the Law in Judgments

When Moses received the Ten Words on Mount Sinai, all the people understood this was the Law of God. Actually the Ten Words set out in human terms what was required in the behavior of man to meet the standards implicit in the nature of God.

As the people lived, they met problems of interpretation in their desire to do the will of God. It was as the people experienced the problems of living that the true meaning of the Ten Words could be thrown into sharp focus.

If two men put forth conflicting claims concerning a piece of property, it might be difficult to accuse either of trying to steal. They were instructed to bring their problems to Moses, who would then judge the equity each man had in his claim.

A man may be hurt in serving another man and claim compensation, since his hurt was directly caused by the labor he was performing for his employer. The employer could certainly deny any intent to harm or to cause harm and thus would feel justified in refusing to pay any sort of damages. The case would then be brought to Moses. Moses would weigh the merits of each claim. He might rule that the employer: (1) should reimburse the laborer for time lost while incapacitated, (2) should perhaps refund whatever cost had been incurred in the treatment of the hurt, (3) should not have to pay extra for non-existent intent to hurt.

These judgments of Moses were then recorded and referred to, as part of the Scriptures, as a guide to other judgments.

To Go Further

When might the violent death of a man not be a violation of the sixth commandment? Is it possible that a workman could be injured while at work and the employer would not be responsible? Explain.

Make a Decision

"But my God shall supply all your need according to his riches in glory by Christ Jesus." This is the confidence the Christian can have because his trust is in God. This promise includes all our needs: both the material needs for our sojourn here and our spiritual needs for our walk with God, so that our lives may be worthy of His name.

As we have seen in our study, God is willing and able to supply our every need, but we must let Him do it. If I refuse to open my hand and heart He cannot fill them. But when I turn to Him He can and will satisfy my every need.

CHAPTER 6

God Lives with His People

Living in faith involves more than being led while making decisions or adopting a plan of action. In order to be able to obey the will of God it is necessary to believe in God, to be aware of Him. In order to believe in Him one must look for Him, and look into His face.

Since God is not visible to the human eye, certain procedures must be followed that will bring the reality of God and the nature of God to the consciousness of man. It is for this reason that men have worship procedures which are so designed that to follow them results in certain definite impressions. In this way comes the growth of convictions which in turn affect the ethical conduct of the worshipers.

Introductory Bible reading for this week: Exodus 25—Leviticus

1st Day   Exodus 29:42-46
"Honored in Worship"

Since God is spirit and is invisible, the procedures of worship must be designed to affect the worshiper in such a way that God is honored. This cannot be done by bringing valuable things to Him. A maid is honored when her lover brings her a diamond ring. A plant manager is honored when his employees give him an expensive car. But God is not sufficiently honored by things we bring with our hands.

To honor God in worship, the soul must esteem God for what He is and appreciate Him for what He has done, is doing and will do. He is over all, and must be esteemed above all else. This is implied by setting aside an exclusive place from which all that is human is kept out of sight. The holy place of the Tabernacle was carefully reserved for certain exercises which symbolized what He did to make worship possible. The holy of holies was set aside in such fashion as to impress upon the worshiper that access to His presence was a rare privilege.

Each article of furniture symbolized an aspect of worship. The priests were carefully clothed and consecrated to do their part in leading the worship exercise. The whole structure of building, furnishings, priests and their duties, actions—all was coordinated in such a way that the worshiper could be aware of the reality of God, the holiness of God and the conditions under which a sinning man could have fellowship and communion with a holy God.

The ritual, which was administered by the Levites, taught the worshiper about the grace of God, showed him what God had done for him and assured him of the blessing that was freely bestowed upon him in the name of God.

It was a profound blessing to know that the creator and the sovereign of the universe cared about each one who came to Him, and that He sought fellowship with such who worshiped Him "in spirit and in truth."

To Go Further

What was so fitting about having the worshiper first sacrifice his offering at the altar? What lessons are suggested by the location of the laver? Why should we think the details of the Tabernacle have significance for understanding true worship? (See Hebrews 9:1-14.)

2nd Day   Exodus 32:15-24
"No Other Gods"

Man cannot bring an offering to God as though he were giving God anything not already rightfully His, inasmuch as God made all things and gave them into man's hands in the first place. Also God is spirit and has no need of material things (Acts 17:24,25). But man can remember what God has done for him and can give God praise and thanksgiving in gratitude (Hebrews 13:15).

Man knows he is dependent because he is constantly using things he did not make, and is always facing circumstances over which he has no control. But man is not always so sure that all comes from the hand of God. Man is tempted to think there are other sources of origin and other powers of control. In this way he dishonors his maker.

This tendency in man's mind to think of other gods to whom he should give some attention and from whom he could expect some help is wrong and is unacceptable to God (Exodus 34:12-17). Such is the common practice of the heathen. One may retain a measure of illicit self-esteem in avoiding total dependence upon the one giver of all things. But certainly there is a demoralization of the person when there is no longer one God to whom praise and thanks should be given (Romans 1:21-25).

When God revealed His Law in the Ten Words, He indicated the first requirement man must face was that all glory belongs to God. In being thankful for benefits received and in seeking more help, man must keep in mind the truth that there is "no other God." By way of emphasizing this, God said of Himself "The Lord . . . is a jealous God" (Exodus 34:14).

Israel manifested the heathen tendency while Moses was on Mount Sinai for forty days. Since God is invisible to the human eye, and Moses had been absent for so long a time, the people prevailed upon Aaron to make them a god which they could see. The cultural influence of Egypt was reflected in the making of the golden calf. The people turned to this idol of their own making with enthusiasm and joy.

Moses demonstrated the anger of God against this idol worship by breaking the tablets of the revealed Word of God upon the rocks and by stern disciplinary action against Aaron and the people.

To Go Further

Why does the human heart seek other gods to glorify? What effect may it have upon a person's mind when he believes that there are a number of gods? How does the world today tend to influence our idea of God?

3rd Day   Exodus 35:25-29
"As the Lord Commanded"

The worship of God should be practiced in a way that is worthy of God. Such a way can be discovered only by revelation. A pattern of worship was shown to Moses on the mount (Hebrews 8:5). Detailed instructions were given as to the design of the Tabernacle, the articles of furniture, the materials to be used, even to the workmen who should supervise the construction.

The Tabernacle was to be built according to the pattern revealed from God, but it was to be made out of materials that would be supplied by the people. The selection of the material and its specific use would be set forth in the revelation of the will of God, but all the material would be brought as a freewill offering by the people.

Because he believes in God, man should willingly

bring all that he has that he might offer this to God for whatever use God will choose to make of it. The men of Israel brought items of gold, silver and precious gems. The women spun cloth to give because their hearts "stirred them up."

The building of the Tabernacle has a profound lesson for all who would worship and serve God. The plan of God gives man the privilege and opportunity of being a co-worker with Him. When his heart is rightly affected, man is moved to bring the very best he has to give to God as a gift. His proper humility is seen in this case in that he gives without any attempt to direct the use of his gift, God Himself being the director of this.

God supplies the design. But the actual carrying out of that design is put into the hands of a wise master builder who will be able to fulfill the will of God (Exodus 35:30-35 and I Corinthians 3:10).

To Go Further

What can a willing worshiper bring to God today? What lessons should a believer today learn for his service unto the Lord from the building of the Tabernacle? What function should the Bible have in the life and work of a believer today?

4th Day   Leviticus 5:5-10
With Offerings

In all the procedures of worship a wonderful

truth to be celebrated over and over is that God will forgive and cleanse sins. But great care is to be taken that the worshiper understand and remember that his redemption and deliverance from sin is due to the amazing grace of Christ, who suffered unto death to remove the guilt and who was raised from the dead to deliver the believer from sin's power.

In the book of Leviticus there is detailed instruction as to the proper procedures to be followed by the worshiper before the coming of Christ. Moses described different offerings, designating each to be related to different needs in the spiritual life of the worshiper.

Each offering in the form of some living animal or bird was to be most carefully selected as being "without blemish." When the creature was put to death, its blood was to be sprinkled upon various elements involved in the worship procedure, including the priest who performed the ceremony, and the items of furniture in the Tabernacle. This prefigured the truth that the sinless Son of God died for sinners, that they might come before God without any guilt or blemish.

The worshiper was to identify himself with the offering so that his sins were to be put upon the sacrifice. When the lamb was killed, the worshiper was to be reckoned as freed from the guilt of his sins.

One offering was to be brought that was made of meal. This seems to symbolize the faithful deeds performed by the believer in obedience to the will of God.

To Go Further

In what ways did the lamb serve to show forth the work of Christ? What is the meaning of the phrase "the blood of Christ"? Do you feel any sense of resentment that your justification before God must be accomplished by someone else and not by you yourself? Explain.

5th Day   Leviticus 10:1-11
In the Right Way

The worship of God on the part of the Old Testament believer involved the observance of certain revealed procedures which would lead the mind of the worshiper into a proper appreciation of the being and works of God. Certain actions were to be performed by the worshiper in a certain way.

It is possible to do what is right in such a way that the result is all wrong. A weed can be killed by swinging the hoe viciously to chop it off by the roots. But the hoe can be swung in such a way that the bean plant is chopped off with the weed, thus defeating the very purpose of hoeing the weed.

Nadab and Abihu were responsible to offer fire upon the altar in the course of their priestly services. They were to do this in a frame of mind that was worthy of the importance of what was being symbolized. Details are not given, but it is reported that they offered "strange fire" upon the altar.

When fire leaped out of the altar to destroy them,

Moses instructed Aaron and his other sons not to mourn the death of those two. By such conduct they were to imply to all the people that the destruction of Nadab and Abihu was proper because of their failure to honor God in what they were doing.

The lessons in this incident are very grave and far-reaching. Ministers and leaders of public worship bear their testimony to the reality and the majesty of God in their leadership in public worship procedures. It is extremely important that all public handling of the testimony of what God has done for man should be soberly and earnestly performed so that all who see may be rightly impressed with the character and the power of God.

To Go Further

Does it make any difference as to how worship services are led? Why?

What is your reaction to a worship service that does not mention Jesus Christ or what He has done?

Name some components of true worship.

6th Day   Leviticus 11:43-47
All Must Be Clean

The only worthy response to God's commands a believer can make is obedience. When a man knows what the will of God is, it goes without saying he should do it. Two conditions can hinder his doing what God wants him to do. A man can indulge himself in laziness and fail to obey because he does not want to exert himself to that extent. This may show up as some form of self-protection. Or a man may be committed to carry out his own ideas without regard to God's desires. In either case this is sin.

In order to teach the children of Israel the importance of right conduct as against wrong conduct, Moses introduced the idea of "clean and unclean." When anything or any action was acceptable to God, Moses called it "clean." When anything or anybody was not acceptable to God, Moses called that "unclean." In this simple way he sought to make the children of Israel aware that their actions and their conduct mattered to God.

The idea of "clean and unclean" was applied to all aspects of their daily life and culture. Some food was clean, some was unclean. The people were instructed to eat only the clean.

The same idea was used to refer to other conduct. Certain rules of equity, justice and charity were set forth as "clean"; violations were classed as "unclean." Always the promise was given that God would bless the "clean," and the warning that God would judge the "unclean."

With all the instruction as to what was considered as "clean," Moses warned what would be the judgment of God upon the "unclean." But this was followed again and again by careful instruction as to what could and should be done about the "unclean." There was always provision in the grace of God for the cleansing of the "unclean."

To Go Further

Name some "unclean practices" today.
How does one go about correcting these?
What is the best antidote?

7th Day   Leviticus 24:5-23
In Orderly Fashion

Doing things in an orderly way commonly reflects both obedience and meekness. At the very outset it shows self-control and in its course it shows a true humility. Also it shows the practical result of knowing the will of God.

God is a God of order and not confusion. This means that God wants things recognized for what they are, and wants everyone to treat them as such. He wants each thing put in the place where it should be, and expects this to be done as His will is more clearly known.

In order to impress upon the children of Israel the importance of obeying God, Moses exercised discipline in several drastic situations. The whole matter of obeying God is truly one of life and death. Thus when a man cursed God and was consequently stoned to death, a tremendous impression would be made upon the people on the vital importance of obedience.

The observance of the Sabbath, in days and years as well as on special occasions, showed that a certain orderly setting aside of one seventh of all time is in the will of God. A regular schedule of other religious activities also may be a source of great blessing to the believer.

Moses did not let the matter rest by revealing the promise of blessing for all who would be obedient. He made a point of warning the disobedient and the careless that God would not hold him guiltless who failed to carry out His will.

To Go Further

How does following a schedule show humility?

How does obeying instructions show self-control?

What can be learned from being orderly in one's work?

Make a Decision

One of the greatest blessings a person can experience is in knowing that God is with him—that he does not have to make it on his own, that he does not have to trust his own wisdom or strength to know and do God's will.

To know this great truth one must be aware of the presence of God. This is why Bible reading and prayer are so important to the Christian. Here he meets God face-to-face, is strengthened and given guidance and assurance that God is with him. "Come boldly unto the throne of grace, that we may obtain mercy, and find grace to help in time of need." Have you been coming often and regularly to the throne of grace?

75

CHAPTER 7

God Orders His People

The gospel promises that God will bless His people. Blessing will mean that living will go on in spiritual security with satisfaction. The believer will have peace and joy. Nothing that hurts or destroys will ultimately trouble those who belong to God. This is the blessing of Abraham that will come to all his seed forever.

The actual form which such blessing takes will depend upon the circumstances in each case. The Scriptures do not describe in detail what will happen. All such blessing will occur as the believer is in the presence of God and obeys His will. God will Himself bring the blessing to His people by His own wisdom and strength.

Introductory Bible reading for this week: Numbers

Order is essential to being. This is seen in the structure of anything. A cathedral is composed of physical elements which, if gathered in piles without order, would be classified as rubbish. To build the cathedral required that the stones be gathered and processed into certain shapes that would fit together according to the architect's design. The metal parts had to be mined and produced to fit into that design. The glass had to be produced by skilled workmen to serve a specific function. Then all the parts had to be assembled and built together by craftsmen who would follow the architect's guidance. Out of this process a structure would result that would serve the purpose of the builder.

Even so with plant organisms. All the chemical elements in a tree are taken from the environment and arranged in the physical form of the tree in such a way that existence is continued and the species is reproduced. This pattern is unchanged in all units of this species.

A similar condition is true even in the case of man. If any variation occurs in the arrangement of the parts or in the proportion of the elements, there is sickness and disease, even death. What is true physiologically may well be true psychologically and sociologically.

This great truth was taught to Israel by the arrangement of the tribes around the Tabernacle whenever Israel stopped in their journey and made camp. An orderly pattern was set up with three tribes on each of the four sides of the Tabernacle.

Despite the fact that such an arrangement left no room for self-determination in choice of position or function, there was peace and order which in turn produced quietness and confidence. There is a profound truth to be seen here about living. The presence of order makes for peace and for joy because of the absence of contention, conflict or confusion.

To Go Further

How is the importance of order to be seen in the operation of an automobile engine?

How is the importance of order to be seen in the matter of health?

Applying the principle to your own habits, what aspects of your life could be changed for the better?

2nd Day   Numbers 8:20-26
In Worship

In worship the believer comes to God to think about Him in a worthy way. Since God is invisible the worshiper cannot contemplate the person of God in a physical way. He can only be mindful of His glorious attributes and of what God has done, is doing and will do.

Being aware of what God has done can arouse appreciation, but if this emotion does not express itself in some act, it can fade away with no real significance to the worshiper. But if this appreciation is expressed in some offering that is presented to God, it will remain longer in the memory. When that offering is expensive so that it is a large matter to the worshiper, then the appreciation actually grows that much larger. To offer a lesser sacrifice will reflect less appreciation.

Moses instructed each of the Hebrew tribes to bring an offering in worship. This would mean individual participation and reflect individual appreciation. By directing that each tribe would bring an offering that was as large as each of the other tribes, Moses left the definite impression that "God is no respecter of persons."

Because sin would disqualify a person from coming to God, it was important that the priests making the offering should be free from guilt and cleansed from sin before they approached the presence of God.

The Christian can rejoice in knowing that Christ Jesus serves as his priest to come before God for him. Jesus of Nazareth had lived a sinless life and so did not need to bring a sin offering when He came to present Himself as the offering on behalf of His people (Hebrews 7:26-28). Since Christ died for all men, each believer can come to God with confidence knowing that with the offering of his heart he brings as much as anyone else can bring. At the same time no one need be tempted to pride with any feeling of superiority; his offering is no more than that of any other believer. At the foot of the cross the ground is level.

To Go Further

When a number of people bring gifts, what are some of the normal tendencies?

What effect does it have upon the soul to realize the offering required is fixed?

3rd Day   Numbers 9:15-23
In Leadership

Living by faith manifests a yielding to the guidance of God. It is not simply a matter of being committed to the ultimate purposes of the will of God. The believer is not left to his own devices in his own judgment to arrive at the goals God plans for him. Not only is the outcome in the will of God, but the procedures leading to that end are prepared and provided for the believer so that his progress to the desired end can be assured.

The leaders of Israel were taken from among the sons of Aaron, these being of the tribe of Levi. These men were not chosen because of superior intelligence or deeper insight. The fortunes of Israel were not dependent upon what the people could do in themselves. These priests were instructed carefully by the Lord Himself, and made their contribution by being faithful in obedience to the revealed will of God.

When any question of proper procedure was raised, Moses sought the mind of the Lord, and then instructed the people. Moses served as the responsible supervisor of all that was done. But Moses made no judgment according to his own ideas. He came to God in prayer to learn God's will and then showed this to his fellow leaders, who in turn showed the people what to do.

The people at times complained about the road they were led to travel. Such complaining was displeasing to God, because in murmuring against their circumstances they were actually murmuring against God. After all it was God's guidance that was given to the people through the leaders. The children of Israel may have thought they were complaining against Moses, but actually they were complaining against God, since He was directing them through Moses.

To Go Further

How should a Christian understand his personal circumstances?

Would accepting all things as being in the will of God destroy ambition? Explain.

4th Day   Numbers 14:36-45
In Obedience

Living by faith demands exact completion of whatever task is given in the will of God. There will be times when a leader will communicate the will of

God about specific conduct, but there will be times when an assignment will be given for which the believer must exercise himself in deciding what to do.

After Moses had led the children of Israel across the desert for the space of about two years they came to a place called Kadesh-barnea. At this point he directed them to "go in and possess the land." Apparently they were to assume some initiative as to performance.

The first action they took was to send out spies, who would scout through the land of Canaan. When these spies returned they brought data about the situation they would face as they entered the land. They would come to high walled cities and would encounter soldiers that were giants. Their own inability to overcome such opposition discouraged them. They decided they could not undertake the task.

Joshua and Caleb were not blind to all the data they had discovered and they recognized their own weakness. But they were also mindful of the power of God who had promised to fight for them. They urged the Israelites to go forward in faith. "If the Lord delight in us, then he will bring us into this land." Despite this exhortation the people acted in unbelief and failed to perform the task given to them.

This incident came to be known as "the provocation" (Hebrews 3:8,9), and resulted in the postponement for a whole generation of the realization of the will of God. None of the people who failed to obey the demands ever entered into the fullness of the blessing which had been set before them.

To Go Further

Why is it important that an adolescent should be given opportunity to exercise his own initiative in conduct?

What are some decisions made by an adolescent that permanently affect his life?

5th Day   Numbers 16:28-35
In Responsibility

Living by faith may involve the believer in the responsibility of leadership. When a number of persons are to do things in common it is important that their actions be so led that there will be unison in the activities of the group. This will require that some serve as leaders. A believer may find that he is given the task of leading others in the will of God.

Among the leaders there are levels of authority, so that when a person is in charge of others to direct their actions, he will at the same time be directed in his leadership by some other leader. This can lead to the temptation of resentment of the one who has the higher authority. Such resentment is actually a form of the sin of pride, and must be condemned and repudiated for the welfare of the group.

Moses, under God, was in charge of all leadership in Israel. Each leader was given a certain authority and a certain responsibility. Korah began to resent the authority of Moses and to complain that Moses took too much authority for himself. The record shows that Moses sought guidance from God at every point in the carrying out of his duties. But the pride of Korah tempted him to challenge Moses openly in his work as leader.

This disorder among the leaders was dealt with sternly. Moses told all Israel, "Hereby ye shall know that the Lord hath sent me to do all these works; for I have not done them of mine own mind." Then he predicted how Korah and his sympathizers would be destroyed. It happened exactly as Moses said it would.

When the children of Israel saw this, some complained that the punishment for this rebellion was too severe. Again the judgment of God came upon them, and was stayed only by the intercession of Moses. But even so 14,700 more died. "Rebellion is as the sin of witchcraft" (I Samuel 15:23).

To Go Further

Why is the rebellion of a leader so dangerous?

What does the incident with Korah teach about the influence of a leader?

How does this lesson apply to society today?

6th Day   Numbers 24:5-9
In Conflict

Living by faith will move the believer unavoidably into conflict with those who are hostile to the will of God. When such opposition occurs there is to be no yielding for the sake of outward, superficial peace. "There is no peace, saith the Lord, unto the wicked." If man opposes man there could be yielding or compromise, but when man opposes God there is no compromise possible.

Such conflict leads toward the destruction of those who oppose the will of God. Apparently God would be eager to guide all men in His grace. He is "slow to anger, and plenteous in mercy." But He is always God. As such He is entitled to the deference and the obedience of all men. To be sure, not all will obey Him to their benefit; some will foolishly oppose Him to their hurt.

In the actual conflict those who oppose the will of God will strive against God's people. Arad of Canaan came out to fight against Israel and was destroyed. Sihon, the Amorite, came out against Israel and was destroyed. Og of Bashan came out against Israel and was destroyed. In no instance was any victory of Israel due to their strength or ability. God entered into every battle to give the margin of victory to His people. But in each, Israel was called upon to fight the enemy. Belonging to God does not mean escape from warfare.

The most dangerous enemy encountered at this period of Israel's history was Moab under their king, Balak. This man saw the record of what happened to Israel's enemies during battle, and thus planned to defeat them by a nonviolent strategy. He sought the help of a prophet named Balaam whom he hired to curse Israel. While Balaam was unable to do anything but bless Israel as he prayed, he did

help the Moabites by showing them how to seduce
Israel through false friendship.

The drastic and violent action of Phinehas, in exe-
cuting judgment upon open flagrant sin, aroused
Israel to a realization of their danger. In the ensuing
battle the enemy was defeated and Israel was set
free to follow the will of God.

To Go Further

Would there ever be a time when to refuse to
fight would be disobedient to God?

What are some dangers for Christians today in
being friendly with ungodly people?

7th Day   Numbers 27:15-23
In Administration

Living by faith includes careful arrangement of
all affairs. It is a mistake to think that living as led
by the will of God is in any sense haphazard. While
it is true that the mind of man does not plan nor
direct the course of affairs, it is by no means true
that what happens is spontaneous or casual. Actually all matters are under careful control.

Just as Moses had been chosen by God to serve as
the leader of the exodus of Israel from Egypt, so
Joshua was chosen under God's guidance to succeed
Moses in his role of leadership.

Through Moses the people were given careful instruction about the offerings they should bring. Ex-

plicit details left the impression their worship activities were really important. In like manner carefully detailed instructions were given for the observance of vows. Any man coming to God was to be careful in his coming and in remembering to do exactly what he had promised.

Relations with other people were to be carefully supervised. The Midianites had become a threat by their friendly approach in which they had lured the children of Israel into pagan and evil practices. A definite repudiation of all that was pagan was to be carried out by destroying the Midianites.

When Reuben and Gad requested special privilege as to locating their inheritance, Moses took special care to guard against unfairness which would have weakened the morale of the nation. By careful regulation and appropriate special requirements, the request of Reuben and Gad was granted in such a way that others would not be hurt.

When the land was divided among the tribes there was careful attention to avoid even the appearance of injustice. Each tribe was assigned certain land as their own but the whole operation was handled in a way that protected the equity of each. The careful selection of the cities of refuge showed an effort to emphasize charity for all, even the wrongdoer.

To Go Further

Why is careful planning consistent with godliness?

What is the common peril in all administration?

How is careful planning related to the guidance of the Holy Spirit?

Make a Decision

The blessing of God is offered to all men: "Whosoever will may come," is the gospel invitation. However, this great blessing can only be fully realized in the lives of those who commit the ordering of their daily lives to God.

The life so ordered by God is a life of peace, joy, satisfaction and blessing unspeakable. This is offered to you today. Do you "know" this fullness of life in Christ Jesus? Jesus Christ said, speaking of abiding in Him, "These things have I spoken unto you, that my joy might remain in you, and that your joy might be full." Are you abiding in Christ?

CHAPTER 8

God Brings His People into Rest

The promise of God to Abraham included a place of peace and rest in which blessing would abound. The plan of God included the bringing out of the Israelites from Egypt, their redemption from bondage and their deliverance from their enemies. This plan led to a destiny in Canaan where the promises of God would bring rich blessing.

When the generation that came out of Egypt failed to enter the land of promise through unbelief which generated disobedience, God ruled that it would never enter. But when the next generation was ready to enter, Moses gave special instructions so that these Israelites might avoid the mistake their fathers made. Upon his death, Joshua became the leader who would bring them into blessing.

Introductory Bible reading for this week: Deuteronomy—Joshua

1st Day   Deuteronomy 4:5-10
Heritage from the Past

The life of faith has a history that can be used to point up ways in which blessing may be gained. The promise of God is always a call to come into His will, that the soul may be blessed. What this will actually mean in personal conduct is not always clear. But noting what has happened in the lives of others it is often possible to see what should be done and what should be avoided.

Moses was leader at the time when Israel came out of Egypt. He had led them across the desert. At Kadesh-barnea he had given them the task of going in to possess the land which God had promised to give to them.

He had seen how they failed to go in because of unbelief. He had continued to be their leader through the thirty-eight years of hopeless wandering and dreary complaining. He had seen the daily manna from heaven and the guidance of the cloud by day and the pillar of fire by night. He knew that God would keep His word according to His promise regardless of their repeated disobedience.

Moses had led them past the land occupied by Moab and Ammon, and guided them to avoid conflict with these people who were their blood kin, being the descendants of Lot. Then he had led them into the land of Sihon, the Amorite, whom they defeated and destroyed in battle. After that they encountered Og of Bashan, whom they also defeated and destroyed. In all this the Lord had been faithful to give them victory.

Such a history should have strengthened the faith of Israel to know that the Lord was their God, and that He could be counted on for guidance and for help. They should have gained a new regard for His law and should have been minded to obey His judgments in everything.

To Go Further

What encouragement could a Christian gain from a knowledge of church history?

What warning could a Christian receive from a knowledge of church history?

How can the study of the biography of Christians be helpful to a believer?

2nd Day   Deuteronomy 8:1-6
Lessons from the Past

Living by faith is marked by special occasions when God reveals His will in some classic way that will always serve to guide the believer. There will always be incidents of stern chastening, when the believer learns God will not tolerate disobedience.

Moses had received the Ten Words on Mount Sinai as the law of God and had accepted the responsibility of teaching that law to the people. He knew profoundly that if they kept the law they would be blessed, but if they disobeyed they would be cursed.

Moses had been so anxious that the Israelites

would remember the law of God and follow it, that he arranged special reminders to help. They were to teach their children daily, talking about what God wanted them to do at all points in their routine activities. They were to wear frontlets on their foreheads between their eyes and on their hands. They were to write the law upon the walls and upon the doors of their homes so there would be a constant reminder of the will of God. And they were to be ready to tell the children the story of how God had delivered them out of Egypt.

Living by faith would result in blessing, but there would be the temptation to take credit for any success that marked their affairs. Moses warned the Israelites to remember it was God who gave them every victory and urged them to give God the glory so the benefits could continue.

As they entered into the land of Canaan, they would come face to face with pagan ideas and the worship of idols.There would be the danger of their taking up such false ideas as their own. Moses urged them to remember that they owed everything to God and to repudiate and destroy every false notion.

To Go Further

What are some of the helps for spiritual life that Christians have received from the past?

What can parents do to help their children believe?

What are some popular notions Christians should repudiate and actively oppose?

Guidance for the Future

Living by faith is marked by obedience to the will of God. Obedience includes knowing what is His will, and then doing it because it is His will. The significance of obedience is not always immediately self-evident. It is not always obvious to a child that the parent's way generally brings the best results. For this reason it is practical to provide certain immediate rewards and punishments to help distinguish between good and bad behavior.

When Moses had carefully reviewed for Israel what God wanted them to do, he was faithful to point out that disobedience would bring certain punishment at once. He spoke of setting before the people "life and good, and death and evil" (Deuteronomy 30:15). To emphasize this, he set forth both the blessing and the curse.

Moses knew that because of their sinful natures, the children of Israel would on occasion do what was evil. Because of this they would be punished. But he knew too that in their distress they would remember God and call upon Him. God would in grace hear their cry of distress and would bring them back to Himself.

Moses predicted that in bringing them back, God would change their inner natures. He would give them a new heart and put within them the disposition to seek His will and to obey it willingly. This pointed forward to the new covenant which every Christian shares in Christ Jesus.

Living by faith presents the prospect of being

controlled from within by God Himself. Such believers do not have a special privilege to do less than the holiness of God would require, but they do have the wonderful advantage of not being dependent upon themselves. It is God "that worketh in them to will and to do of His good pleasure."

To Go Further

How is the Bible a help to a Christian?

How is the Holy Spirit a help to a Christian?

In what sense is Christ our Saviour, if we must still obey the Word of God even after having placed our trust in Him?

4th Day   Joshua 1:1-9
Principle for Progress

Living by faith involves a deliberate response on the part of the believer to the Word of God. At the beginning the Word comes in the form of an invitation which is to be obeyed when the soul comes to the Lord in humble acceptance of the salvation God offers to him. But as the believer grows in the knowledge of God and His will, there is a later stage of maturity in which the Word comes as a directive.

The believer is told what to do and obeys by moving out and doing God's will on his own initiative. In the raising of a crop it is true that God "giveth the increase" and that without His blessing all

94

activity would be barren, but it is also true that the farmer must sow the seed. Paul must plant and Apollos must water so that God, in blessing, can give the increase.

This truth was demonstrated in the career of Joshua. He was called to take up the leadership which Moses had borne, and was promised that God would be with him as he was with Moses. The life of Moses was marked by exceptional obedience; his greatest title will always be "the servant of the Lord." Joshua was to serve in that same way, but this would include obedient exercise of his own initiative in doing what God commanded.

God gave to Joshua a profound principle which will always be a part of the life of faith. God told Joshua, "Every place that the sole of your foot shall tread upon, that have I given unto you."

This promise is a challenge to the believer today. The land will be his if and when he takes it. To put the sole of his foot upon it requires an obedience in response to this challenge. He needs to leave behind what he has had and step forward into potential opposition and trouble, that he might gain that which is promised.

To Go Further

What may hold a person back from moving forward in God's will?

What may a person face today that would discourage him from accepting Christ?

How could anyone ever have the strength to forsake all that he has now for the sake of something promised?

5th Day   Joshua 4:4-11
Decision in Action

Living by faith is an ongoing affair very much like going on a journey. Abraham was called to move. He was to come out of his own country, his own people, into a land that God would show him and give to him. This would be a new land where he had never been before. This is the classic pattern of living by faith.

In their wandering in the desert, when Israel came up to the point where they were to enter into the land, they received special instruction as to what they were to do.

The crossing of the Jordan was an amazing feat, made possible only by the help of God. The dividing of the waters when the river was in flood was a major miracle. But the significance of this event in the history of Israel was even greater. When Israel crossed the Jordan the nation launched a course of action that could never be undone. They entered the land once for all, for better or worse.

There is a profound lesson in this event for all who would accept the call of God to live by faith. After due preparation, there will come a time when action must be taken openly. After a time of courtship the wedding will be the decisive act that sets in motion the life of marriage.

The life of faith may have an obscure origin in one's experience, as to just when faith in God began to function, but it is to be expected that sometime there will be some sort of actual commitment that will always be significant as something decisive. When such commitment can be associated with some overt act like responding to an invitation, appearing before a church to be received as a member, or bearing witness as a professed believer in Christ, it can become a notable event in the history of a soul.

To Go Further

Why could the response to an invitation at an evangelistic meeting be a decisive moment in the life of a believer?

Why is it often true that the spiritual life of a person who grew up in an atmosphere hostile to the gospel is deeper than that of one raised in a Christian home?

6th Day   Joshua 7:6-13
Obedience for Victory

At times the life of faith comes into situations where conflict is unavoidable. The circumstances may be such that victory is nowhere in sight and the believer seems doomed to defeat. But God is a living God and can give guidance in the course of the battle that can bring victory. The one thing the believer can do is to obey implicitly whatever he is told to do.

When Israel came to Jericho, they found a situation that seemed altogether impossible. The high walls would withstand any kind of assault the children of Israel could possibly make. But God directed that they should march around Jericho once each day for six days and seven times on the seventh day. When this was completed, they were to shout. This they did and the walls fell down. This was victory through faith, in which all the glory belonged to God.

When the Israelites moved on to Ai, they expected an easy victory. But they were defeated. When Joshua in dismay went to God in prayer, he was told there was sin in the camp and God would not bless Israel with victory until the sin was confessed and cleansed by judgment. Joshua discovered that Achan had disobeyed instructions and had taken some of the loot at Jericho for himself. Achan was put to death that the sin might be purged. Then Joshua led the people in a second attack upon Ai, and this one was successful. Once again victory was given in response to obedience in faith.

When the men of Gibeon came to Joshua and pretended to come from a great distance, they humbly begged for a treaty that would spare their city. Accepting their lies as truth because of the manufactured evidence they submitted, Joshua in good will granted their petition. But this was a mistake. The record tells that Joshua had not sought guidance from the Lord in this matter.

To Go Further

What lessons can be learned from the fall of Jericho? What lessons can you learn from the defeat at Ai? What are your fiercest temptations and how are you meeting them?

7th Day   Joshua 24:14-25
Commitment for Rest

The life of faith embraces the promise of finding peace and rest. Such blessing is promised as a result of obedience. "Take my yoke upon you, and learn of me; for I am meek and lowly in heart: and ye shall find rest unto your souls" (Matthew 11:29).

The land of Canaan had been promised to Abraham and to his seed. But the land was occupied by the Canaanites who claimed it was theirs. Thus conflict was unavoidable, and Israel had to fight for what had been given to them in the promise of God. In this conflict the Canaanites were to be destroyed so that Israel could live in peace and have rest.

Joshua pressed the campaign for the conquest of the whole land. When he realized that he would not live to see the task completed, he planned the whole campaign and assigned areas to the respective tribes and arranged cooperation among those who would be neighbors.

When Reuben and Gad proposed to build a second altar on the east side of Jordan, Joshua took steps to insure the future solidarity of the twelve tribes. Their peace and rest depended upon their united strength, and they would resist division with all the vigor at their command.

As Joshua came to the end of his days he could foresee the peril that Israel might be influenced to adopt pagan ideas about God. In order to withstand this danger Joshua challenged the people to a positive commitment to worship the God of Abraham, Isaac and Jacob. In a dramatic ceremony he led them to a public committal of themselves to be forever faithful to their God.

To Go Further

What lessons about total consecration can be learned from Joshua's plan to conquer the whole land?

What lessons for spiritual life can be learned from Joshua's action about the second altar?

Make a Decision

Salvation is the work of God done in, by and through Jesus Christ. It is God's purpose to bring us to Himself. He wants us in His presence, to fellowship with Himself forever. This is the ultimate of all that God does in Christ Jesus. This rest and blessing is available here and now if we will receive it.

Just as God led the children of Israel into the Promised Land of rest and blessing, even so, He will lead us here and now into the land of promises in Christ Jesus. Do you know this rest and blessing in your personal life?

CHAPTER 9

God Chastens His People

The life of faith passes through stages of growth and maturity similar to natural living. The believer begins as a babe with little knowledge or self-control. At this stage he eagerly receives what the grace of God will give him, and rejoices in the goodness of God. As he develops he begins to learn what he should do and begins to feel his own capacity to select what he wants in the will of God.

Soon he is given some responsibility to exercise his initiative. The temptation will come to follow his own wishes rather than the will of God. Such disobedience must be discouraged lest the whole life be ruined. When suffering is inflicted to turn the believer away from disobedience it may be called chastening rather than punishment.

Introductory Bible reading for this week: Judges

1st Day   Judges 1:17-33
Faulty Obedience Endangers

Living by faith includes the responsibility to perform certain tasks. When the will of God is revealed, it is important that it be carried out exactly as directed. The believer may not always recognize the importance of what he was given to do and so may stop short of complete obedience. Such an omission may later cause real trouble.

Total attention to all aspects of what is assigned is necessary for success. When a surgeon removes a malignant tumor it is essential that all of it be taken out. Leaving any part may prove fatal. "For whosoever shall keep the whole law, and yet offend in one point, he is guilty of all" (James 2:10).

When the Israelites moved in to possess the land of Canaan, they were instructed to destroy the Canaanites totally. In actual performance each tribe stopped short of complete obedience. The record is written about Judah that they "could not drive out the inhabitants of the valley, because they had chariots of iron." This is not worthy of the history of an Israel which was under God's guidance and help. Years before Moses had proclaimed "The Lord your God . . . shall fight for you." When Judah allowed the Canaanites to remain because they could not drive them out, it was because of their unbelief.

The record continues to show this blemish of incomplete obedience. "The children of Benjamin did not drive out the Jebusites." "They let go the man and all his family." "Neither did Manasseh drive out the inhabitants of Beth-shean and her towns." "And it came to pass, when Israel was strong, that they put the Canaanites to tribute, and did not utterly drive them out." "Neither did Ephraim drive out the Canaanites that dwelt in Gezer." "Neither did Zebulun drive out the inhabitants of Kitron." "Neither did Asher drive out the inhabitants of Accho." "Neither did Naphtali drive out the inhabitants of Bethshemesh." Later history would show how disastrous these failures to obey completely turned out to be.

To Go Further

Give some of the reasons for this failure to obey completely?

Do you ever use any of these reasons for explaining incomplete obedience in your own life?

2nd Day   Judges 2:11-23
Chastening the Wayward Restores

Living by faith does not mean that the believer will always obey. Even when he is committed to obey God there may be times when he will fail. This may not always be due to a passive sort of weakness. The believer can be wayward and disobedient at times.

However, God will not allow the disobedient to pass without treatment. It is so easy when a soul has once failed to obey God, to disobey again and again. It is most important that the wayward soul should be restored to fellowship with God and to obedience. For this reason God will bring distress upon the wayward to show the dire consequence of turning away from God.

When the Israelites entered the land of Canaan they were given their assignments and told to destroy the inhabitants. We have noted that they failed to obey and compromised by allowing some of the Canaanites to remain in the land. In his overruling providence God made this very circumstance into a means of chastening. Whenever the children of Israel forgot the Lord and began to worship the gods of the Canaanites, God allowed the Canaanites who had been spared, to bring the Israelites into bondage and distress.

In their misery Israel would return to God and cry out for His help. God would send a judge who would show the people the error of their ways and lead them in repentance to worship God in truth. Then the judge would lead them in revolt against their oppressors. God would bless and give them victory. Then the land would again have peace.

Because He knew that in their human waywardness they would slip into this error again and again, God did not bring about the utter destruction of the Canaanites. Even though they were reduced to the status of servants they were always a potential threat to the freedom of the Israelites.

To Go Further

How may trouble help the spiritual welfare of a believer?

105

What are some of the possible consequences of a Christian's disobedience to the Holy Spirit?

3rd Day   Judges 3:5-11
Deliverance Is from God

Living by faith is marked at times by serious trouble which develops because of wayward disobedience. The trouble seems quite proper because of the wrong conduct of the believer. The outlook at such times would be bleak indeed if the believer had only himself to turn to for deliverance. But it is to the glory of God that the record shows that God provides the deliverance when the soul in trouble asks for help.

The first trouble developed when the children of Israel intermarried with the Canaanites who lived among them. It followed quite naturally that they would begin to worship their gods, and soon they "did evil in the sight of the Lord . . . their God, and served Baalim and the groves" (Judges 3:7). "Therefore the anger of the Lord was hot against Israel," and He "sold them" to become slaves of the king of Mesopotamia. This would seem to be a fair result of their foolish conduct. But when they cried to God, He heard them and sent Othniel to be their judge and deliverer. Following this the land had peace for forty years.

After Othniel died "the children of Israel did evil again in the sight of the Lord." Because of this "the Lord strengthened Eglon the king of Moab against

Israel." After being defeated in battle "the children of Israel served Eglon the king of Moab eighteen years." "But when the children of Israel cried unto the Lord, the Lord raised them up a deliverer, Ehud, the son of Gera, a Benjaminite, a man left-handed." Ehud employed real deception to enable him to get close enough to Eglon to kill him. This he finally accomplished. "And the land had rest fourscore years."

To Go Further

How is the mercy of God seen when trouble comes to the disobedient?

How is the love of a parent involved when a disobedient child is punished?

How may the grace of God be involved when a Christian loses his job?

4th Day   Judges 6:7-16
Call to Serve Is from God

Living by faith involves the believer in fellowship with other believers. The will of God is often communicated through some one of the group who becomes the spokesman for God to the group as a whole. When believers are wayward they may be in need of a special message from God. In His mercy God calls someone who is willing to be obedient and shows him what the will of God is. This one becomes a servant of God with a mission to tell others what should be done.

When Israel forgot their relationship with God and followed the pagans in the worship of their gods, God allowed the Canaanites to overcome the Israelites and to bring them into bondage. In this condition they would suffer distress until they cried to God for help. God would be faithful to His promise and would send a servant of His to lead the children of Israel back into obedience. The blessing of God would not come until they had changed their ways by breaking fellowship with the Canaanites, by turning away from idols, and by once again obeying the word of the Lord.

At a time when the Midianites were oppressing Israel and destroying their crops so that the people were greatly impoverished, the children of Israel cried to God for help. An angel was sent to call Gideon to the task of leading the people back to God. It was hard for Gideon to believe that God was any longer interested in the welfare of Israel because of the distress on every side. But the angel convinced him that God would truly be with him if he would lead a revolt against Midian.

The career of Gideon was begun by an overt act of violence in which he smashed the idol which the Midianites had set up on his father's farm. The people were ready in heart to follow his dramatic leadership to complete victory over Midian.

God first persuaded Gideon of his call to leadership to the point where he acted upon it. Then he was ready to lead the people.

To Go Further

Is widespread disaster and distress a sign that God has forsaken His people?

What lesson can be learned here for a believer who is aware of a general lack of blessing?

5th Day   Judges 11:24-40
Integrity in Service Is from God

Living in faith includes serving God by helping others. God calls persons to Himself and to communion with others who also believe (Matthew 18:20). Such fellowship in the group needs leadership within the group. Pastors, teachers, personal workers, and the like, serve by helping others to know the will of God and to do it.

When the group recognizes the service such a leader gives there may be real gratitude and sincere appreciation. There may also be a readiness to give some reward as a token of appreciation. There will then be a real temptation for the leader to seek personal profit and thus to do his work out of an unworthy motivation.

When Gideon had led Israel to victory upon victory in achieving their deliverance from their enemies, the people asked him to be their king (Judges 8:22,23). Gideon wisely refused their request. In this he was obedient to the guidance from God which he had followed throughout his career.

In the days of his leadership Jephthah contended with the forces of Ammon. In the heat of battle

109

Jephthah vowed a vow that if God gave him victory he would sacrifice to God the first living creature he met on his return home. It happened that this was his daughter. Although he was the ruler over all the forces of Israel, Jephthah would not seek an escape from his vow. His daughter also urged him to be faithful and to keep his vow even though it meant the loss of her life. Such integrity had a profound effect upon all Israel.

Integrity among leaders contributes mightily to the welfare of the nation. It is part of the service which the leader gives as he obeys the will of God. Despite his favored position of being over all others in the nation, the leader has his personal responsibility to God. Temptation is even harder to withstand because the leader is not subject to any fellow believer. The only way he can be safe from error in this situation is by keeping close to God in fellowship and obedience to His calling.

To Go Further

What improper advantages might a pastor take to himself because of his position?

What are some temptations that will come to a person who is ministering the gospel to others in distress?

6th Day Judges 16:25-31
Strength in Service Is from God

Living by faith will include occasions when the course to be followed will demand a great deal more strength than the believer has in himself. Instead of turning back the believer will look up to God for help and find strength for what he is called to do. What he does may be so remarkable that he may win fame as an exceptional person. But the wise believer knows "power belongeth unto God."

Samson was born under unusual circumstances. His parents understood very well that his birth was directly an act of God. Early in life he began to display extraordinary physical strength.

In following his own desires Samson became involved with an evil woman, Delilah, who lured him to confide in her and disclose the secret of his strength. Because he trusted himself to her, he was taken captive by the Philistines. They put out his eyes and made him a slave to do their bidding. It gave them much pleasure to abuse him and ridicule him in public. But in all this God was working out His will in an amazing way.

On one occasion the Philistines made sport of Samson at a large public gathering. His great strength had been restored to him, but this was not known by his captors. In his blindness he asked the boy that guided him to let him lean against the pillars supporting the building. In this way he could get his hands on the uprights that carried the weight of the crowd gathered to jeer at him.

Then Samson prayed to God for strength such as he formerly had. In this God-given strength he pulled down the pillars so that the whole structure collapsed. It cost him his life, but in this he served Israel by slaying more of her enemies in death than he had in life.

To Go Further

What should a believer do when the task in hand seems more than he can do?

Should a believer ever refuse to accept a task because it is too difficult?

7th Day   Judges 21:16-25
Order in the Nation Is from God

Living by faith will result in the providence of God overruling the selfish actions of men to bring His will to pass. Even when the big decisions have been made in line with the revealed will of God, there will often be in lesser matters actions inspired by selfish wishes. These seem to be in the area where men are challenged to exercise their own initiative to do the will of God. Here they have a measure of freedom, and in sinfulness they can choose to do as they please. Such action, however, is still under God's supervision and He is able to make even the wrath of man praise Him.

In the latter chapters of the Book of Judges is the record of a number of incidents marked by the selfish desires of men, which were overruled to serve some good purpose. The making of the ephod in Micah's house was involved with theft and selfishness. But providentially a Levite came by and was taken in to lift the religious practices of that home to a proper level. Later the men from the tribe of Dan came and violently seized the ephod and the priest, and took them along. Despite the fact that these men of Dan seized the city of Laish with violence, they were able to build their own city and set up the ephod and the priest which they had captured to have their place of worship.

When certain wicked men of Benjamin criminally assaulted a woman until she died, all the children of Israel assembled to punish these men. When the men of Benjamin refused to turn over these wicked men for punishment, a fierce battle was fought and the tribe of Benjamin was almost destroyed.

Some six hundred men of Benjamin escaped, but later everyone realized the tribe of Benjamin would die out unless these men could find wives and establish families. By arranging to allow the men of Benjamin to kidnap young women of the town of Shiloh, this difficulty was overcome. The whole affair was marked by wrongdoing, but God seemed to overrule in all this to bring His will to pass.

To Go Further

What lessons can be learned from this portion of Scripture about the providence of God?

How can a Christian live confidently day by day?

If God in providence can overrule the selfish actions of men, does that mean such actions will not be judged as sin?

Make a Decision

"Be not deceived; God is not mocked: for whatsoever a man soweth, that shall he also reap" (Galatians 6:7). It is to the peace and safety of the believer that God will not allow him to go on a selfish way without dire consequences. God will stop him in his tracks to make him aware of the seriousness of his actions. True, not all suffering is due to waywardness in one's soul, but he will know whether his heart is pure before God or if he has been following his own desires and ambitions. It is to the glory and praise of God that when the wayward soul cries unto the Lord, He will hear him and deliver him out of all his fears. How is it with your soul?

CHAPTER 10

God Provides a King

Living by faith requires leadership. God is invisible and His ways are past finding out. When the children of Israel started on their exodus from Egypt, journeyed across the desert and entered into the land of promise, they first had Moses and then Joshua, who told them what God wanted them to do. In time, leadership appeared in the three separate functions of prophet, priest and king.

The prophet would tell God's people what God wanted them to hear. The priest would approach God on behalf of the people and bring to God what the people wanted Him to hear. The king would coordinate the activities of the people by seeking to bring about a unified obedience to the will of God.

Introductory Bible reading for this week: I Samuel 1—15

1st Day | Samuel 1:9-18
God Answers Prayer

The life of faith will confront some situations that seem unbearable. The circumstances may be aggravated by personal feelings, but the distress is just as real. Because the soul believes in God, petition will be made for help in some form of relief. Sometimes the burden is so definite, the petition will be specific. Prayer will be made for a specific answer. It belongs to the glory of the infinite God of mercy and grace that He will hear such a personal plea and answer with the very blessing that has been asked for.

Hannah was one of two wives of her husband and was troubled because she was barren. She came to worship God and began to pray that He should cause her to give birth to a male child.

In praying, Hannah humbled herself and committed herself to give the child to God for His service, if God would but grant her plea. When she was misunderstood and falsely accused of being drunk with wine because she prayed so earnestly that she uttered words audibly, though engaged in private prayer, Hannah was meek. She humbly explained that her conduct was due to the weight of her burden. Eli assured her that her prayer would be granted.

When the child Samuel was born, Hannah kept her vow. When he had been weaned, she brought him to the house of God and gave him to Eli that he might serve Eli while being trained in the service of the Lord. All of this is an eloquent testimony to the grace of God, who will hear the cry for help that originates in a very personal need, and will answer the petition of the humble soul.

Samuel grew up to be one of the greatest men of God in all the Scriptures. As his own ministry drew to its end, he anointed Saul to be king. After Saul disqualified himself through disobedience, Samuel anointed David to be king in his place. Samuel is one of the few servants of God of whom no evil is recorded.

To Go Further

What lessons on prayer may a believer learn from Hannah's experience? In what way was Hannah's attitude toward God revealed in this incident? Was Hannah selfish in her praying?

2nd Day   I Samuel 2:27-3:12
God Calls an Obedient Person

Living by faith includes the call of God to His service. Responding to the call of God is something that needs to be learned. This is of the greatest importance in relation to child training. If a child learns to respond obediently to any call from those who are in authority, that person will find it easier to respond in obedience to the call of God. There is the danger of being misled, but this is unavoidable in this world.

Samuel had been brought to Eli when he was a

young child. Something of his training can be seen in his immediate response when he heard his name called: "Here am I." With this as a basis already established, Eli could instruct him further to say, "Speak, Lord; for thy servant heareth." There was no involved argument necessary, neither were any reservations implied as to what limits Samuel would put upon his obedience. Apparently he was prepared to follow wherever he was led.

Young as he was, Samuel was given an idea of the service he was to perform throughout his life. He was to receive the word of the Lord Himself and obediently share it with others.

Even though it would seem that Eli failed to train his own sons, there is reason to believe that he gave Samuel the right kind of upbringing. Often in Scripture there is the record of God calling to His service a man who needed to be changed to be useful as a servant. Samuel seems to have been brought up "in the nurture and admonition of the Lord." There is no indication that there was ever a time when he was not obedient. His outstanding career is forever an evidence that coming to the Lord in childhood, with no wasted years of misspent willfulness, is not a handicap to a devoted, effectual ministry (see II Timothy 3:14,15).

To Go Further

Compare the call of Timothy to that of Samuel (Acts 16:1-3). Compare the childhood of Samuel to that of Joseph (Genesis 37:1-14).

Weigh the benefits to a minister of a background like that of Samuel as compared to that of the apostle Paul.

3rd Day | Samuel 5:1-7
God Will Not Give His Glory to Another

The life of faith at times encounters instances when disobedient persons seek to use the things of God to their own advantage. A man may be committed to walk in the ways of God and yet lapse into unbelief when he tries to make his way in his own wisdom and strength. With high regard for the Bible as the source of truth and with all due respect to its prestige, there may be times when a man will seek to use it to support his own personal ideas.

In the days of Samuel the Ark was a symbol of the leadership of God. Time and again the presence of the Ark had implied the support of the living God unto victory. The sons of Eli were not godly men, nor did they serve in obedience to the will of God. But when they engaged the Philistines in battle, they sought to turn the tide of battle from defeat to victory by bringing the Ark into the midst of the fighting men. Thus by their own devices they sought to manipulate the power of God to their own ends. But the Philistines won the battle and captured the Ark.

Apparently God would not allow unbelieving men to make use of His power at their own will. Though it meant that Israel would be defeated at the hands of the pagan Philistines, God would not compromise Himself to save His people from defeat.

But this did not mean that the Philistines could profit by possessing the Ark. Actually, handling the Ark in an irreverent way brought disaster upon the pagans. They did not know what to do with it, but they were sure they needed to get rid of it. The whole record clearly demonstrated that God will not let His glory be taken over by anybody.

To Go Further

What shall we think of anyone who uses the Bible as a means to winning a personal argument?

What lessons are here for the man who would join a church (1) to help his business? (2) to get elected to political office?

What are some ways in which a group of young people might act as did the sons of Eli (I Samuel 4:4)?

4th Day   I Samuel 7:3-12
God Blesses Sincere Repentance

Living by faith can include periods of time when the heart of the believer is divided in loyalty between devotion to the Lord and attachment to popular ideas current in the world. At such times the spirit is weakened and there is no victory. Although the believer belongs to God and has been benefited by the blessing of God in times past, there can be a certain acceptance of the gods of the land. As long as this is the case there can be no triumph or joy in the Lord, but rather distress and bondage.

In times like these the faithful preaching of God's prophet can challenge the people to repent and to turn to God with all their hearts.

Samuel was the preacher who called Israel to put away the false gods of Baalim and Ashtaroth and to serve the Lord only. He arranged a special gathering of the people when he would lead them in prayer. As he preached the law of God to them, the people fasted and poured out their hearts before the Lord, saying, "We have sinned against the Lord." News of this public prayer meeting came to the Philistines, their masters, who came in force to put down any threat of revolt.

The children of Israel feared the Philistines and cried unto Samuel that he should continue to pray for them that the Lord might intervene on their behalf. Samuel led them into complete consecration by preparing a burnt offering as he cried to the Lord for help. The Lord did help by sending a severe thunderstorm upon the Philistines which so "discomfited them" that Israel could win the battle. The Philistines fled in defeat as Israel pursued them out of the country. Samuel then commemorated their victory with public thanksgiving to God.

In this whole event is to be seen the classic pattern of revival. God always blesses sincere repentance with victory and joy.

To Go Further

How does preaching function in promoting real revival?

What part does praying have as people turn to God?

Why would anybody oppose repentance and revival in others?

5th Day   I Samuel 8:4-10
God Grants the Request of the People

The life of faith can falter at times through popular demands for procedures that are inspired by the trend of affairs in the world outside. Such requests may be quite unacceptable to the faithful spiritual leader, who can see the dangerous aspects in them and recognizes their origin in the influence of pagans who do not even pretend to serve God. But God may surprise and dismay His faithful servant by granting popular requests and directing the servant to heed the demands of the people.

The elders of Israel came to Samuel to request that he make someone to be king. The nations around them had monarchies that seemed to work out very well.

The popular request for a king displeased Samuel. He recognized that it was a modish request inspired by the desire to be like other people. He did not feel that following the example of unbelievers was worthy of the people of God. And he could see the danger of monarchial abuse of authority.

But he would not answer their request on the basis of his own feeling or judgment.

Samuel was astonished to be told by the Lord that he should grant their request. God gave him to understand he was not wrong in his appraisal of their waywardness in making this proposal. It was only too true that they were turning away from Samuel, but actually their fault was even deeper than that—they were turning away from God. This was the constant tendency that had always lurked in the children of Israel.

However, Samuel was to let them know the danger of their course. He was to grant their request, but he was to warn them of the risk they were taking. This would be a real test of the obedience of Samuel as a servant.

To Go Further

What lessons are in this incident for a pastor?

Are there parallels in this account with modern ecclesiastical developments? Explain.

What can be the source of assurance for an older person who sees his advice being ignored?

6th Day I Samuel 12:10-15
God Provides a King

Living by faith does not assure infallibility of judgment. Even though they may have a deep dependence upon God and a real regard for His leadership and help, God's people may in the exercise of their own choice (in their own judgment) actually do foolish things. But God does not interfere with their decisions, even when they are mistaken. He does, however, let them experience the results of their actions that they may learn from them.

Acting upon the guidance given to him by God, Samuel anointed Saul as the first king of Israel. When he presented Saul as king, the people were not yet fully prepared to give him their allegiance. Samuel reminded Israel of the true nature of their request, that it was contrary to his own advice and dishonoring to God. Then he brought them the king they had requested.

Saul showed his leadership ability in waiting for a crisis in which to step forward and assume command. He led the people to victory in battle with the Ammonites, and as a result, was popularly received and acclaimed as king.

When Saul was thus firmly established in the hearts of the people as king, Samuel made a public withdrawal from his long time place of leadership in the nation. Once again he reviewed the disobedient spirit which inspired their request for a king, and set out his argument as to why they had not needed to follow this popular trend. Then he showed them how they could avoid the danger, and how the king himself could secure the blessing of God. The people were smitten by the truth of what he said and freely admitted that he was right in his appraisal of their waywardness. They humbly asked him to pray for them.

To Go Further

What lessons can a pastor learn from Samuel's experience?

What lessons can parents learn from this whole development?

What value could there be in Samuel's reminding the people of their waywardness in calling for a king?

7th Day I Samuel 15:16-23
God Judges Disobedience

Living by faith allows a person some degree of freedom of choice. Just as any response may vary according to the will of the servant, so is the obedience of a believer to the call of God. When the call is to come, the servant may come promptly, slowly, running, or limping, according to his eagerness to please or his physical condition or the road he is traveling. So when a servant is told to go and do a certain work, there is a variety of ways in which that work can be done. It is within this possibility of variation that a servant may be more or less pleasing to the master.

When Saul was crowned king he was put in a position where he could command a wide variety of procedures in carrying out his responsibilities. Certain principles could guide him to do what was acceptable to God. It would be in the use or the neglect of these principles that Saul would be acting in obedience or disobedience to God.

When Saul gathered his army to fight against the Philistines at Gilgal, he was to wait for Samuel to offer sacrifices to God to seek blessing upon the venture. Samuel was delayed in coming, and Saul was obliged to wait seven days before attacking the Philistines. Finally in impatience, Saul offered the sacrifice himself.

Samuel appeared immediately after Saul had acted so presumptuously. He told Saul that in this he had forfeited his opportunity to establish himself and his descendants after him as king. Even though he was king, and all the more because he was king, obedience to God was absolutely essential. Military advantages might be sacrificed, but obedience to God was essential. Saul's action showed he was depending upon his own wit and strength for victory —this is not the way of faith.

To Go Further

What exactly is wrong about one's being so busy he does not have time to pray?

What lessons can be learned here by the Christian who is so busy he does not have time to go to church?

What can be learned here about the providence of God in delaying His help?

Make a Decision

As Israel of old needed a leader, we need someone to guide us day by day and, thank God, we have in Christ Jesus the guide who will never leave us nor forsake us.

We must make Jesus Christ our king if we want to live under his leadership and blessing. When Jesus Christ reigns, all else must be cast aside. He cannot share His throne with another. *Christ must be Lord of All or He will not be Lord at all.* Is He your Lord and king? What is His chief competition in your life? He wants to be yours so He can bless you and lead you into joy and peace.

CHAPTER 11

God Blesses His King

Living by faith includes receiving assignments to be fulfilled and tasks to be performed. While basically obedience to the will of God is like a child responding to being led by the hand, actually the will of the believer is involved in controlling self and situations to bring the will of God to pass. The problem of self-control requires discipline of body, mind, heart and will. The person must rule over himself and take charge of the situation to be obedient to the will of God.

In this respect the believer must actually be a king in his own being. Much of the truth revealed in the Bible about what God required of the king of Israel is actually a revelation of what God requires of the mature believer.

Introductory Bible reading for this week: I Samuel 16—II Samuel 7

1st Day   I Samuel 16:11-18
The King Is Called

Living by faith includes being called to serve God
in responsible conduct of all the affairs put under
the control of the believer. It must be understood
that the opportunity for service is a gift of God, and
that the believer is responsible to God for the way
he handles the situation in which he is in charge. In
a definite way he must sense his commitment to his
task. And he needs assurance that God will bless
him as he serves in obedience.

David was only a lad tending his father's sheep
when Samuel came to anoint him to become king
of Israel. Though he had already performed feats of
courage and skill in protecting his father's sheep, he
was still too young to be counted as one of the men
in the family and too young to serve in the army.
Samuel was led to take him aside and anoint him for
this great responsibility.

Despite his personal prowess and skill David was
not given any serious responsibility when he was
brought into Saul's service. His first assignment was
to play the harp that Saul might be refreshed.

Later David came to bring supplies to his brothers who were in the army and heard Goliath issue
his defiant challenge to the Israelites. David could
not understand why some believing Israelite did not
accept the challenge. When he commented on this
he was asked if he was willing to meet Goliath, and
immediately indicated he was eager to do so. His
readiness was reported to Saul who authorized him
to represent Israel in the duel. Saul offered to lend

David his armor, but he wisely refused and put his confidence in the sling he had learned to use while herding sheep. Picking five smooth stones, he went out to meet the giant. Goliath was insulted that a mere lad was sent to meet him in battle, but David told him he was facing the God of Israel who would deliver him into David's hand.

To Go Further

What does this incident teach about the age at which life commitment can be made?

Is it adequate to say that David's courage enabled him to meet Goliath with confidence? Explain.

2nd Day | Samuel 17:45-51
The King Is Tested

Living by faith will bring a believer into situations where his confidence in his being in the will of God, and in the power of God to help him, will be severely tested. If he can be confident he is in the will of God, he can be assured God will help him. If he can be confident of God's power, he can rest assured in his ultimate victory. God in His providence will lead the believer into situations that test his confidence in order that the believer's assurance may be confirmed by actual experience.

When Saul was anointed to be king, he was tested

in battle with the Philistines. When David was anointed, he was tested in his duel with Goliath. When David faced Goliath, the disadvantages of David's youth, size and equipment made the help of God very necessary. David met this test of his faith with implicit confidence in God. He faced Goliath without any uneasiness because his confidence was centered in God, not in himself.

When David slew Goliath he was immediately thrust into a situation which tested him as to whether he would take any of the glory to himself. Popular ballads emphasized the outstanding acclaim the public gave to David. This made King Saul jealous, and he eyed David to see if there were any reason he could bring David to grief.

David behaved himself wisely in public so as not to agitate Saul's opposition to him. When he was called in to play the harp for Saul, he was alerted to the peril of being killed by him. David became a close friend of Jonathan, but, wisely, he did not trust Saul. When he realized how determined Saul was to kill him, he fled from the palace and became a fugitive. As Saul pursued him he had repeated opportunity to kill Saul but he would not raise a hand against the Lord's anointed.

To Go Further

What lessons can we all learn from David's actions toward Saul?

What special dangers beset a preacher who has been blessed in his ministry?

If a man really trusts in God, should he flee from danger? Illustrate from Joseph's life.

3rd Day   I Samuel 20:24-34
The King Is Rejected

Living by faith includes being called to special tasks of responsibility. With each responsibility are privileges which allow considerable freedom of choice and liberty in conduct. Such freedom could be a temptation to willful behavior which would be displeasing to God. Self-willed conduct can only be avoided through self-control which has been established through discipline. The believer may be led through dangerous situations in which he avoids destruction only by humble denial of his own personal feelings. Such a response to peril, which he escapes by fleeing, involves denial of pride and strengthens his self-control.

David had known since he was a lad tending sheep that God had chosen him to become king of Israel. In that position of privilege he would naturally be tempted to pride and self-will. Yet it would be most important that the king act in moderation and in obedience to the will of God. As king, David would encounter opportunities to exercise his own choice such as he had never known. Nothing in his life as a child or youth would have prepared him for the perils his new privileges would present. Thus God in His providence led David through certain trials that prepared him in a special way for his great responsibility as king.

Despite his careful and humble conduct before Saul, David realized that he was in danger of his life when in Saul's presence. He knew that Saul meant to destroy him, and by his alert watchfulness he escaped without harm on several occasions when Saul attempted to kill him. But he knew too that he must leave to be safe. Even though he would be classed as a rebel and treated as a fugitive, David knew this was the only course he could take. It would be particularly humiliating for a young man who had been hailed as a national hero to run for his life. But in this very experience David was learning his own personal inability to cope with situations he would face as king—he needed God.

To Go Further

Why would pride be such a peril to a young king? How would personal rejection prepare a man for great privilege? What sort of special temptations confront a soul that has been called to be a child of God?

4th Day | Samuel 25:25-33
The King Is Guided

Living by faith will bring a believer into situations where he can be helped by the wise counsel of friends. The believer can make a mistake in judgment without realizing he is wrong. He may not realize his error and so fail to seek guidance. Because his judgment involves practical aspects that can be seen by others, it is possible that a friend may see his mistake and help him by warning him of the peril of his course.

David knew he was to become king of Israel. While fleeing from Saul he recruited a following among other fugitives and led them as an efficient company of outlaws who made their headquarters in secret hideouts unknown to King Saul. David showed his basic loyalty to Israel by using his band of fighting men to protect frontier settlements from the raiding parties of hostile neighbors. In this role of protector David won sincere support and practical help from grateful herdsmen who realized they enjoyed safety because of David's watchful care.

David called on Nabal, whom he had protected, to give him supplies for his men. Nabal selfishly refused to acknowledge David's past help and actually humiliated David's men who had come to receive food and supplies. David was so angered by this churlish conduct that he gathered his men to raid Nabal by way of punishment.

Abigail, Nabal's wife, heard of David's intention and promptly took steps to guide him into a more worthy course of action. She prepared food to present to David to gain a favorable hearing. When she met the angry leader, she advised him with humble wisdom not to carry out his intentions. Conceding that he had every right to be offended, she pointed out that he was destined to be king. It was impor-

tant that he avoid doing anything that would be unworthy of a king. David saw her wisdom at once
and changed his plans.

To Go Further

When can the advice of a faithful friend actually
be a message from God?

What does this incident show about David himself?

Under what circumstances should a Christian
heed advice from others?

5th Day   I Samuel 30:18-25
The King Is Helped

Living by faith involves being led by the will of
God in every situation as it comes. Sometimes the
believer will face conditions so difficult that he cannot possibly manage in his own strength. Sometimes
God in His providence will overrule so that the believer is actually delivered from his dilemma by
some change in his circumstances. But sometimes it
turns out that help is brought through someone who
is actually not personally involved in the believer's
affairs. In all of this the hand of God is active in arranging matters to help the believer in what he
must do.

David was finally so hard pressed by Saul that he

fled into exile in Gath, where he allied his followers with the king of the country to help him in his warfare with his neighbors. Since all the nations involved were potential enemies of Israel, David could in good conscience fight to defeat any of them.

But when Achish, king of Gath, engaged in warfare with Saul, David was faced with an intolerable situation. He had never struck a hostile blow against Israel. His dilemma as to how he could maintain himself as a loyal ally to Achish and not fight against Israel was solved when Achish dismissed him for security reasons. In this way David was spared from a break with Achish, and from fighting his own people.

While David and his men were in the army of Achish, their home city of Ziklag was raided and plundered, and the families taken prisoners. David's own men turned against him and blamed him for this disaster. Once again David turned to God in prayer. A sick Egyptian who had been left to die by the invaders told David where they were so that David could promptly pursue them and rescue the captives. This was done and once again David was established as a great leader.

To Go Further

When would a believer ever need help from men?
Recall experiences in which you have been helped by unbelievers.

What lessons for a believer can be learned from
this aspect of David's career?

6th Day   II Samuel 3:17-21
The King Is Victorious

Living by faith brings the believer into situations
where he must control and direct himself and his re-
sources to be blessed. He will meet problems he
cannot solve and face issues that demand more than
his strength and wisdom. Despite the liberty he will
feel in his movements and the freedom he has in his
choice, he will not be able to cope with what
threatens to destroy him. In all this he will learn
that he is dependent upon God for help that he
might be blessed. For God watches over the believer
and is able to so affect the situation that victory is
assured.

David had a strenuous career of real difficulty
after he had been anointed to be king of Israel.
Deadly opposition from Saul had threatened his life
and seemed to prevent him from ever entering into
what he had been called to do. When he refused to
harm Saul personally, even though his own life was
at stake, it seemed that he would never enter into
the kingdom for which he had been anointed. But
God had promised to bless him and this was his
hope.

David had refrained from raising his hand against
Saul. But in the providence of God, Saul went into
battle with the Philistines and was killed. Without
any effort on his part, David was delivered from the

opposition of Saul. But David made it very clear that he had no personal pleasure in the death of Saul. He wrote an ode to Saul's memory and publicly mourned for Saul. He punished those who had dishonored Saul after his death.

The house of Saul under Ishbosheth, led by Abner, fought against David. Abner was a capable foe and much damage could have been done to Israel by this civil war. But when Ishbosheth showed himself to be a foolish king, Abner came to make peace with David. David welcomed him and agreed to end hostilities.

To Go Further

How shall a Christian act when his opposition is removed by death?

Why is public opinion important to a believer?

7th Day II Samuel 7:8-17
The King Is Blessed

Living by faith will include times when the believer is specially blessed with favor from God. This will not mean that the believer will presume that God will bless him in any case regardless of his conduct. But it does mean that the believer is encouraged to do his very best, being assured that God will then bless him richly in one way or another. God will do more than the believer can ask or think in helping him to a pattern of conduct beyond anything he could ever do for himself.

When the rebellion of Saul's supporters had finally been put down, David was crowned king over all the nation of Israel. He immediately led an assault upon the stronghold of Jerusalem that this might be the center of his administration. After his capital city had been secured, David continued to extend his control to establish his government both within Israel's boundaries and among neighboring nations.

As soon as David had completed the establishing of his rule he wanted to build a permanent place of worship in which to honor God. From the time of Moses when Israel was a nomadic people moving from place to place, the place of worship had been a tent called the Tabernacle. Now that the people had settled in permanent homes, and Hiram, king of Tyre, had built David a palace, David felt it was a fitting thing that a permanent Temple should be built to the glory of God.

Nathan the prophet was sent by God to David to tell him that his intention was known to God and appreciated. However, since David had personally been involved in so much warfare, he would not be allowed to build the Temple. This honor would come to David's son, though David could contribute to that building by gathering the materials that would be used.

But David was now given a covenant that promised that one of his seed should sit on the throne forever. Furthermore, his rule should spread over the whole earth until all the kingdoms of the earth should accept the seed of David as king.

139

To Go Further

Of what advantage to David's rule would be the obtaining of Jerusalem for his capital?

What does David's desire to build a Temple indicate about his relationship to God?

What lessons can be learned from the fact that David was not allowed to build the Temple?

Make a Decision

The blessing of God is promised to all who put their trust in Him and follow Him in obedience to do His will. God not only calls the soul to Himself; He also guides and helps the believer to victory.

The believer does not have to depend upon his own strength or wisdom to bring God's promises to pass in his personal life. This God will provide! He delights in blessing those who trust Him. "Trust in the Lord . . . and lean not unto thine own understanding. In all thy ways acknowledge him, and he shall direct thy paths." His direction always leads into blessing. Are you trusting your entire personal life to Him? Can you think of any unsurrendered areas where you are counting on your own understanding to see you through?

CHAPTER 12

God Is Served by His King

Living by faith involves receiving the Word of God as commandment, as a directive guiding the course of conduct.

The believer is called to be a king in all aspects of his life which involve the exercise of his choice and control. He is to take such matters in hand and employ them in the will of God. The very private matter of himself as a person is perhaps the most important item he must handle. "He that ruleth his spirit [is better] than he that taketh a city" (Proverbs 16:32). The king must have dominion over his own heart if he ever wants to serve God successfully.

Introductory Bible reading for this week: II Samuel 8—24

1st Day II Samuel 8:9-15
The King Secures His Throne

Living by faith involves the consistent performance of the believer who has developed a strong
control over all phases of his responsibility. In God's
plan the believer is given a task to perform and a
certain freedom of choice and liberty of action in
which to achieve his personal way of doing the will
of God. Just because he has this liberty and this
freedom, he is threatened by others who will seek to
oppose his plan. In order to perform efficiently and
to achieve the success he needs, the believer must
bring the entire area of his responsibility under his
actual dominion.

When David had finally been confirmed as king
over all Israel and had received the covenant from
God that one of his seed should be on the throne
forever, he took practical steps to establish his dominion for efficient service. Among the neighbors of
Israel were some nations which were hostile enemies and had seized certain lands that once belonged to Israel. These foes David dealt with indi-
vidually in succession, defeating them in battle and
forcing them to pay tribute so that they actually
contributed to the effective government of Israel.

Some of the neighbors were friendly and helpful.
These were properly honored and their help was
used to aid in establishing David's rule. In the entire area where David's dominion extended he took
steps to make sure that all would be kept definitely
under control.

The believer may find that in his obedience to the

will of God there are elements in the world about him that present a definite threat to the success of his purpose. These can be controlled, however, and be made actually to serve his cause. Though potentially a threat, by careful control they can be turned into an asset. Some of the other natural elements do not threaten any difficulty; these can be immediately incorporated and used to advantage.

To Go Further

What are some of the natural elements that threaten the believer's blessing and how can they be controlled?

What are some natural elements that do not hinder obedience to God and how can they be used?

Why is it so important that a believer should have strength of character?

2nd Day   II Samuel 9:7-13
The King Shows Grace

Living by faith involves other people. Some of the people with whom the believer has dealings may be related to those whom he is under obligation to serve. This may lead to further obligations. When the believer has finally established his personal control over his situation and actions, he should use this control in the service of others.

At the time they established their mutual pact of friendship, Jonathan asked David when he eventually became king to remember his household and deal with them favorably. David did not forget his friend or his covenant. When his throne was finally secured, David enquired if there were not some of Jonathan's people around to whom he could show "the kindness of God."

Mephibosheth was the crippled son of Jonathan and was living in poverty and despair when he was identified and brought to David. Nothing about Mephibosheth himself made any difference to David. What he was doing, he was doing for Jonathan's sake, and for his word's sake. He restored all his property and even made him a member of the king's household.

Such action on David's part did not originate naturally from David's heart. It was directly the outgrowth of David's own experience of the grace of God. So with the believer in his relations with other people. There is a sense in which the Son of God has an interest in all men. It was for them He died. It is to them the believers are sent by our Lord's great commission (Matthew 28:18-20). The nations of the world may not have an appeal to the believer that he should expend himself to bring them the gospel. And the believer himself may not have any natural disposition to put himself out to tell them the gospel. But the Lord has commanded this to be done. When we surrender to God, we covenant to be obedient regardless of the cost. But in obedience to Him we find the only true freedom. And in telling the Good News we find joy unspeakable.

To Go Further

Draw out the implications of the parallel between this action of David and obedience to the great commission?

What aspect of the parable of the sheep and the goats is similar to this incident (Matthew 25:31-46)?

3rd Day II Samuel 12:7-14
The King Sins and Repents

Living by faith does not mean that the believer will never sin again. We have before noted that as the believer matures, a certain liberty of action and freedom of choice is given to him in which it will be his responsibility to discipline himself and to control himself to do the will of God. Because this is an area of responsibility, the believer has certain privileges, but this does not give him license to do as he pleases.

David was later to be known as a man who had done all things in obedience to God "save only in the matter of Uriah the Hittite." The story of his sin with Bathsheba is well known. It may not always be noticed that this sin occurred "at the time when kings go forth to battle.... But David tarried still at Jerusalem" (II Samuel 11:1). While this does not condone the sin it helps us to understand how this believing man could fall so deeply, and it warns us concerning conditions that could be dangerous. "The devil always finds mischief for idle hands to do." But no good end will be served by ignoring the fact that David sinned, and sinned grievously.

The faithful prophet Nathan confronted David with the fact of his sin. David immediately confessed it. Nathan promptly assured him of his forgiveness, but pointed out certain dire consequences that would inevitably follow. History has plainly recorded the fulfillment of Nathan's prophecy: the child would die, the sword would never depart from David's family, and the name of God would be blasphemed among the Gentiles. All this happened.

It is a wonderful truth that sin can be forgiven and guilt can be pardoned. But no one should ever overlook the damaging consequences of sin. The prodigal son could change his attitude and be welcomed home as one alive from the dead, but no implication was given that his wasted inheritance was ever restored or replaced.

To Go Further

What warning can a Christian take from this experience of David? How could a man like David fall into such sin? What lessons can be learned from this incident about trusting human nature?

4th Day   II Samuel 14:13-21
The King Shows Mercy

Living by faith will include dealing with persons who will harm the believer and cause him hurt and loss. The believer is not immune to such actions against his person and work. When necessary he will act to protect himself and what he has. But when the threat is past and the peril of loss or hurt is removed, the believer will be led to deal in mercy with his defeated enemy.

David had many enemies in his lifetime but none hurt him as much as his own son. Absalom schemed to destroy his brother Amnon, and when this was done David banished Absalom from his presence. But David in time "was comforted concerning Amnon, seeing he was dead" (II Samuel 13:39). His soul "longed to go forth unto Absalom" who stayed in exile for three years. It was true that Absalom had killed his brother, and later he was to be guilty of plotting to destroy his father, but he was David's son, and David's heart went out to him.

Joab and a wise woman from Tekoah planned an approach to David that was successful in having him relent from his banishment of Absalom. Without any thought of condoning what Absalom had done and apparently with no fear as to what havoc he might cause if he were brought back, the king acted in mercy and lifted the ban to permit Absalom to return.

Often we are prone to feel that mercy should be reserved for those who are worthy. How seldom do we realize that according to such a principle no one would ever receive the mercy of God! Mercy does not come as a reward to some culprit who has, since his judgment, established a very fine record. Mercy comes out of the heart of the merciful. It is given as grace to the unfortunate who are often at fault, not because they deserve it or because they are now going to do better, but because they are in distress and because this is a kindness being shown to them out of a kind heart.

To Go Further

What is the most encouraging aspect of this event to you and to anyone else?

How was the mercy David showed to Absalom like the mercy of God to us?

Considering what Absalom did later, what does this event teach about showing mercy?

5th Day   II Samuel 15:10-17
The King Is Dethroned by His Own Son

Living by faith will not keep the believer from suffering some grievous wounds. "The servant is not greater than his lord." Jesus of Nazareth was perfect. He always obeyed His Father in heaven. Yet He suffered cruelly. The believer expects to suffer in self-denial. He knows he will forego personal desires and will be deprived of all willful pleasures. But he must also be ready to endure the wounds inflicted upon him by his "friends."

David endured many hard experiences in his persecution by Saul and in his battles against the enemies of Israel. But possibly nothing was ever so hard to bear as being dethroned by the rebellion of his own son. After going the second mile in permit ting Absalom to return to Jerusalem, he had to accept the fact that this same son had undermined him with his people and had actually seized the throne. David had no illusions about what Absalom would do to gain his ends, so he fled for his life.

David showed his cunning and his confidence even in retreat. He laid plans as to how he might defeat Absalom's maneuver even while in headlong flight to save his life. At the same time he displayed neither anger nor despair. In the crisis several unexpected friends showed their loyalty even as he showed how concerned he was for their welfare. Despite the grave danger he faced, David conducted himself in every way as a king facing adversity.

It is hard to accept the apparent evil which permeates the whole world and is even to be seen in the intimate circles in which the believer is at home. The reality of sin is obvious everywhere and must be faced by the believer at all times. David was able to deal with evil without panic because he put his whole trust in God. This did not mean that he would relax his vigilance or that he would cease from meeting every challenge, but it did mean that he had a certain quietness and confidence which was the source of his strength. He was able to forego destroying Shimei, for example, because he could leave him to God (II Samuel 16:12).

To Go Further

In what concrete way can you apply this lesson to

your own affairs? Is opposition to a pastor evidence
that he is not serving God?

6th Day   II Samuel 19:9-15
The King Is Restored by Faithful Subjects

Living by faith may bring experiences of great
joy to the believer because of faithful and gracious
conduct on the part of true friends. When Peter
asked Jesus of Nazareth what the disciples could
look forward to that would compensate for the
losses they had experienced when they forsook all
and followed him, the Lord assured them they
"shall receive an hundredfold, and shall inherit everlasting life" (Matthew 19:29). The blessing of the
support of kind friends is a gift from God. It is important that the believer understand their devotion
to him is not because he deserves it. Let him thank
God for His grace that has provided this blessing.

David put his whole trust in God. When his own
son threatened to kill him and seize the throne, forcing David to flee for his life, he was kept strong in
his confidence that God was the Almighty One who
was allowing this to happen, but who would take
care of David in any case. When Absalom had been
defeated and destroyed, David did not at once rush
back to take over the throne. He avoided letting his
own will prompt him to assume this position in any
arbitrary way. He kept in mind that he could only
be king in any real sense through the help of God.
Now he waited for God to move the people to bring
him back to the throne.

David was not disappointed. The people themselves began to urge that steps be taken to bring the
king back (II Samuel 19:20). But even so David did
not remain passive in simply waiting for others to
act. He quietly sent the suggestion through the
priests that they speak to the elders of Israel that it
would be a fitting thing if they led in expressing the
popular demand that David be brought back to his
throne.

To Go Further

Why was it so important that the people request
that David be brought back to the throne?

How does this aspect of the whole affair show the
faith of David?

What lessons can a believer learn from this event
about his own affairs?

7th Day   II Samuel 24:17-25
The King Worships God with Praise

Living by faith should be marked by praise and
thanksgiving to God for his gracious guidance and
help. No matter how much authority has been given
to the believer that he might exercise his will in serving God, the believer must always remember that
all power belongs to God. Without the help of God,
the king could do nothing. Therefore the faithful
believer will praise God at all times and especially

thank Him for His help in times of great achievement.

When David was restored to his throne by popular demand and given unanimous support from all sections of his kingdom, he knew that God had blessed him. When there was famine in the land for three years David knew that something in the national affairs did not please God, and he immediately inquired of the Lord. God revealed to David a wrong that had been done to the Gibeonites when Saul was king. David promptly took action to correct the wrong. The wrong had not been his doing, but it had been done by the king of Israel. He was now king and he would accept the responsibility to make this right.

David wrote a psalm of thanksgiving that acknowledged God's constant help in all that had been done. By taking no credit to himself David gave all the glory to God, and led the hearts of the people in praising God for His mercy and grace.

David as king had accomplished great things, and yet he knew that he did not in himself have the strength to do what needed to be done. God's help was given to David through the heroic support and service of mighty men who were devoted to him. David realized the allegiance of such men was in itself from the Lord and he refused to take any personal advantage from their willing bravery. He publicly gave God the praise and the glory for the great deeds these men performed.

To Go Further

What is the peculiar temptation that can beset a successful servant of God?

What are some of the common dangers that beset veteran believers?

Make a Decision

"Whether therefore ye eat, or drink, or whatsoever ye do, do all to the glory of God" (I Corinthians 10:31). It is the great privilege of the believer to live out his life here in this world in service to God. That is, everything he does is to be under the guidance and control of God. Even to the very way in which he dresses, plays, works, and worships—all can be done as unto the Lord and to His glory.

When Jesus of Nazareth was here He could say: "I do always those things that please Him." How is it with your dress, your play, your work, and your worship? Are these done as unto the Lord?

CHAPTER 13

God Glorifies His King

Living by faith involves the believer in controlling himself and using his environment to do the will of God. Liberty of action and freedom of choice within certain limits are given to the believer as privileges in which he is responsible to obey God in performing certain tasks. God watches over him to give him guidance when he seeks it and help when he asks for it. At all times God is bringing His will to pass in all that is done.

When the believer is faithful to his trust and obedient in his performance, God is glorified. It is then His glorious will so to bless the believer that there is evidence that God is with him.

Introductory Bible reading for this week: I Kings 1—11

1st Day   I Kings 1:28-37
God Permitted the King to Plan the Future

Living by faith includes serving God by controlling and directing personal activity in His will. When God has seen fit to give the believer liberty of action and freedom of choice in which he is to do the will of God, He puts some task into his hands. The performance of this assignment becomes a personal project wherein success or failure is important.

When David was anointed to become king of Israel he was given the task of ruling that nation. Through his lifetime he saw his kingdom established and become strong in promoting peace and welfare of his people. There yet remained need for assurance of national stability after David was gone.

When David became infirm with old age the question of his successor became urgent. He had several sons who might occupy the throne. One of these, Adonijah, coveted the position and planned to usurp the throne while David was still living. Nathan the prophet and Bathsheba, the queen, worked together to bring the facts of the critical situation to the attention of David. The old king knew that the welfare of the nation would be promoted if Solomon, the son of Bathsheba, became king.

David called Zadok the priest to arrange a public induction ceremony where Solomon would be crowned king, and where the message from David would be given to the people calling upon them to support the king of his choice. By this prompt action David forestalled the campaign of Adonijah in that Solomon began to function as king at once. Adonijah fled to the altar in fear for his life, but Solomon was not disposed to harm him.

To Go Further

Why would it be right for David to name his successor?

How does this event with Solomon seem to be parallel with the case of Joshua (Deut. 31:1-8)?

Could Solomon have been God's choice as king? Explain.

2nd Day   I Kings 2:1-10
God Blesses Obedience in His King

Living by faith includes liberty in action and freedom of choice within the will of God. The believer is given a task to perform and is to follow the guidance of God. Within his own choices the believer is to obey God that he might do His will. It has always been true that they who do the will of God abide forever. God encourages obedience by rewarding such conduct with His blessing.

When Solomon was chosen to be king, David gave him counsel to obey the will of God in everything. This would ensure blessing upon his reign. Then David gave him specific advice concerning certain persons with whom he would have to deal.

Solomon as a young man could not possibly have

the knowledge necessary to make wise decisions in all critical situations. David knew of several problems that would confront Solomon immediately, and he knew how they should be handled. David gave Solomon specific instructions to follow in each case. It was part of the wisdom of Solomon that he followed David's counsel in these matters.

David had kept in mind throughout his reign that he was only a servant of God charged with responsibility in the performance of his task. David did not look upon Israel as his possession or upon his throne as his own. He knew all belonged to God. And while he had the opportunity to rule over the kingdom, he remembered that it was God who had put him in that place and who would judge his actions according to truth. And David knew that all this would be the same with Solomon.

To Go Further

How would David's instructions help Solomon to understand his task as king?

What natural temptations would beset a young king like Solomon?

What lessons can a young Christian learn from this stage of Solomon's career?

3rd Day   I Kings 3:5-15
God Grants Wisdom to His King

Living by faith requires wisdom in the exercise of

liberty in action and freedom of choice. As long as the believer is a babe, his only responsibility is simply to obey each specific direction as received. But when he is given a task to perform by his own selection of procedure, the believer needs wisdom to enable him to judge the meaning of the issues before him and to evaluate the significance of the several choices he could make. Good intentions will be important, but good judgment will be necessary for success in what he is doing.

Solomon was young and this meant he was inexperienced. As king he had all the prestige and opportunity for personal action that the throne provided. When God asked him in a dream what he wanted most for help in his tasks, Solomon asked for wisdom. This request pleased the Lord, who then promised Solomon not only the wisdom he had asked for, but also riches and honor so that his reign should be distinguished above all others in its success.

When Solomon awoke from his dream he went first of all to the house of the Lord and publicly worshiped Him. In this way he served notice to everyone that he would depend upon God for guidance and for help.

As king, Solomon would need to act as judge in the difficult problems that needed to be settled among people in his kingdom. Here his youth and inexperience could be a definite handicap. But in the first case brought before him, Solomon was able to make a judgment that was so obviously true that all Israel, when they heard it, recognized that Solomon had been blessed of God with wisdom to perform good judgments. "If any of you lack wisdom,

let him ask of God ... and it shall be given him"
(James 1:5).

To Go Further

What did Solomon's request for wisdom reveal
about Solomon?

Are good intentions ever enough for daily living?

When a Christian prays for wisdom, what does
his request show?

4th Day   I Kings 5:1-12
God Helps His King to Worship

Living by faith depends upon the believer's confidence in God. "He that cometh to God must believe
that he is, and that he is a rewarder of them that dil-
igently seek him" (Hebrews 11:6). Such conviction
is not natural. "Faith cometh by hearing, and hearing by the word of God" (Romans 10:17). The soul
must come to God and look unto Him. It is what the
soul sees in God and in His acts that begets confidence and generates conviction. In worship the soul
looks into the face of God as revealed in Jesus
Christ and is blessed with trust.

The acts of God have been determinative in the
history of His people. But succeeding generations
would not know certain of these acts from experience. For this reason a ritual of worship exercises
was authorized to be conducted first in the Taber-

nacle and later in the Temple. These would represent to the worshipers the truth revealed in the original acts of God.

When Solomon prepared to worship God he planned to build a Temple, and to furnish it as authorized by God and revealed to Moses. In gathering materials for this project he went for help to Hiram, king of Tyre, who had been "a lover of David." Hiram rejoiced to give this assistance, and he became a friend of Solomon even as he had been a friend of David. He provided the timber of cedar and fir essential to the construction of the Temple.

Solomon showed his wisdom by being generous to Hiram. He "gave Hiram twenty thousand measures of wheat for food to his household, and twenty measures of pure oil: thus gave Solomon to Hiram year by year" (I Kings 5:11). In this he laid the solid foundation for "peace between Hiram and Solomon."

It is so very important to remember that in the planning of the worship of God, the personal feelings of everyone involved should be respected and considered.

To Go Further

Why is the worship of God so important in the life of a believer?

What lessons can be learned from the fact that Hiram was not of Israel?

What does this incident teach a worker for the Lord about community public relations?

Living by faith involves definite commitment to
God on the part of the believer. While it is true that
the believer must exercise his faith at all times in a
continuous fashion, it is also true that the whole relationship in faith will profit by definite acts of commitment. This principle may be illustrated by the
relationship of marriage, which is a continuing one.
It is normally preceded by a period of courtship
which may also have been characterized by an un-
broken communion of love for some time. But nonetheless, the wedding ceremony is significant. And
in worship there is tremendous value in the periodic
formal celebration of enduring truths.

Solomon expected to worship God regularly in
the Temple he had built. He meant for his people to
worship God. So he planned and conducted a great
dedication ceremony in which the meaning of this
worship was reviewed and stressed. He set the example himself because he wanted all the people to
share in the celebration, that God might be honored
and they might be blessed.

In his classic prayer of consecration Solomon
briefly reviewed the history of God's gracious dealings with Israel, with David and with himself, praising God for His mercy and His grace. Then the king
listed specific situations in which he prayed God
would be especially gracious. Whenever Israel
would come to prayer, he asked that God would be
gracious to listen and to forgive. In any instance of a
man committing trespass against his neighbor, he

asked that God would judge with equity. If ever Israel were defeated in battle because of sin, and they would come confessing, he asked that God would be gracious to forgive. When the people would come to ask for help in time of drought or crop failure, he asked God to be mindful of their need. Solomon also mentioned other situations, and always called on God to be gracious with His help.

To Go Further

What help is gained by recalling former days when God richly blessed?

Why is it important to be specific in making requests from God?

What lessons can be learned by the Christian in this consecration service?

6th Day   I Kings 9:1-9
God Fulfills His Promises to His King

Living by faith is marked from time to time by great blessing from God according to His promises. When the believer has matured God gives him liberty in action and freedom of choice, that the believer might serve Him in performing whatever task has been assigned to him. In such service the believer acts as a king disciplining himself and dominating his circumstances that he might do what God wants him to do. Although in a primary sense he is personally responsible, the believer remembers God and seeks to please Him. In times of perplexity he seeks God's guidance and in times of weakness he asks God for strength. And yet in a real sense it is his work and he plans to present it to God as his personal offering for God's judgment and approval. When a man's work is pleasing to God, He blesses him richly. This blessing is basically spiritual and is thus most enriching to the life of the recipient.

Solomon had received a great opportunity when he was made king of Israel. When he asked for wisdom he had been especially pleasing to God. In the course of his reign Solomon had been diligent to follow the guidance of God and to employ the wisdom given to him. The result was that Israel was blessed with more glory than they had ever known. In his wisdom Solomon promoted peace with his neighbors which permitted the full strength of his people to be used constructively. The result was an increase in fortune and in glory in all aspects of life.

The Queen of Sheba made a special trip to Israel to see for herself whether the reports she had heard could be true. Her reaction is famous: "Behold, the half was not told me."

Material wealth, general prosperity, peaceable relations with surrounding nations all combined to crown Solomon's reign with honor in abundance. What David had so bravely fought to secure, Solomon wisely developed to serve his people. "The blessing of the Lord, it maketh rich, and he addeth no sorrow with it."

To Go Further

How could the material benefits which enriched Israel under Solomon be to the glory of God?

How are wisdom, peace and prosperity related?

Can the blessing of God for a Christian ever be a matter of material, temporal benefits?

7th Day   I Kings 11:9-13
God Judges the Foolish King

Living by faith does not mean that a believer will never do foolish things. When a believer has matured in the use of God's gifts of liberty in action and freedom in choice, he is actually in danger of doing foolishly. He is somewhat free in his privileges and can be tempted to satisfy his own desires and seek his own interests. This does not mean he has turned away from God entirely, but that he is now using his privileges to please himself. But God does not hold him guiltless. God will deal with him in judgment.

Solomon began his career with every advantage. David had left him a strong government, a great name among the neighboring nations, and a united people. God had blessed him with wisdom as he requested, and had added riches and honor in abundance. By wisdom and diligence Solomon had prospered until his reign was the most glorious in the history of Israel.

"But King Solomon loved many strange women."

And so it happened "when Solomon was old, that his wives turned away his heart after other gods: and his heart was not perfect with the Lord his God, as was the heart of David his father" (I Kings 11:4). Through this tragic intimacy Solomon yielded to allow pagan worship centers to be built in Israel.

"And the Lord was angry with Solomon, because his heart was turned from the Lord God of Israel, which had appeared unto him twice, and had commanded him concerning this thing, that he should not go after other gods: but he kept not that which the Lord commanded" (I Kings 11:9,10).

This is the sad story of man's failure to obey God even under the most favorable conditions. But later in the revelation of God there would come a son of David who would "do always those things that please him."

To Go Further

What does this sad end to a wonderful reign show about the nature of man?

Where did Solomon basically fail?

What lessons are in this for any Christian?

Make a Decision

God has a mind to bless us. He works in us to that end. When He accomplishes His work and actually produces in us the performance of His will as it was done in Christ Jesus, He is glorified in us. "Herein is my father glorified, that ye bear much fruit" (John 15:8).

True, glory will come in heaven, but this can be the Christian's earthly experience also if he will yield himself to God and let God have His way in his heart, to work out His will in his life to the honor and glory of God. Is your life filled with the glory of the Lord as you go about your daily round of duties? If not, what is the hindrance? Are you willing to yield up the obstacle, thus exchanging your poverty for His riches? Today? Right now? To God be the glory.

Books for Further Study

BRUCE, F. F. *Israel and the Nations* (From the Exodus to A.D. 70). Grand Rapids: Eerdmans, 1963.

CRUDEN, ALEXANDER. *Cruden's Concordance.* This Bible concordance is available from several publishers in abridged and unabridged editions.

DAVIDSON, FRANCIS, editor. *The New Bible Commentary.* Grand Rapids: Eerdmans, 1953.

DOUGLAS, J. D., organizing editor. *The New Bible Dictionary.* Grand Rapids: Eerdmans, 1962.

GROLLENBERG, LUCAS H. *Atlas of the Bible.* New York: Nelson, 1956.

HARRISON, EVERETT F., editor-in-chief. *Baker's Dictionary of Theology.* Grand Rapids: Baker, 1960.

HARRISON, EVERETT F. and PFEIFFER, CHARLES F., editors. *The Wycliffe Bible Commentary.* Chicago: Moody, 1962.

HENRY, CARL F. H., consulting editor. *The Biblical Expositor.* Philadelphia: Lippincott, 1960.

HENRY, MATTHEW. *Commentary on the Whole Bible* (in one volume). Grand Rapids: Zondervan, 1960.

KEIL, CARL F. and DELITZSCH, FRANZ. *Commentaries on the Old Testament.* 25 volumes. Grand Rapids: Eerdmans, reprint 1952.

LANGE, PETER JOHN. *Commentary on the Holy Scriptures.* Grand Rapids: Zondervan, 1960.

MEARS, HENRIETTA C. *What the Bible Is All About.* Glendale, California: G/L Regal, 1966.

MICKELSEN, A. BERKELEY. *Interpreting the Bible.* Grand Rapids: Eerdmans, 1963.

PFEIFFER, CHARLES F. *Egypt and the Exodus.* Grand Rapids: Baker, 1964.

PFEIFFER, CHARLES F. and VOS, HOWARD F. *The Wycliffe Historical Geography of Bible Lands.* Chicago: Moody, 1967.

REDPATH, ALAN. *The Making of a Man of God, Studies in the Life of David.* Westwood, N. J.: Revell, 1962.

REDPATH, ALAN. *Victorious Christian Living, Studies in the Book of Joshua.* Westwood, N. J.: Revell, 1955.

The Sacred Land. A. J. Holman Co., Philadelphia, 1966. (Historical maps from before 1500 B.C. to present day.)

SCHULTZ, SAMUEL J. *The Old Testament Speaks.* New York: Alfred A. Knopf, revised edition, 1964.

SCROGGIE, W. GRAHAM. *The Fascination of the Old Testament Story.* London: Marshall, Morgan & Scott, 1930.

SMITH, WILBUR. *Profitable Bible Stuay.* Natick, Mass.: Wilde, 1963.

TAYLOR, WILLIAM M. *David, King of Israel.* Grand Rapids: Baker, reprint 1961.

TAYLOR, WILLIAM M. *Moses the Law-Giver.* Grand Rapids: Baker, reprint 1961.

WHYTE, ALEXANDER. *Whyte's Bible Characters,* Vol. I: *Old Testament.* Grand Rapids: Zondervan, reprint 1962.

YADIN, YIGAEL. *Art of Warfare of Biblical Lands.* New York: McGraw-Hill, 1963.

YOUNG, EDWARD J. *An Introduction to the Old Testament.* Grand Rapids: Eerdmans, 1958.